THE

CRYPTO

SOVEREIGN

Wesley Thysse

For Brenda, Ad and Hugo.
For showing me what freedom is, and isn't...

<Copyright and Limitations_

Title:	The Crypto Sovereign
Version 1.1:	Independently Published
Type:	Paperback, November 27, 2020
ISBN:	9798551443766

<Foreword_

I am writing to you from ~~Pokhara, Nepal~~. From the roof of my guest house, I see the snow-covered peaks of the ~~Himalayas~~—gorgeous towering mountains over eight kilometers tall. But I cannot go there. You see, on account of COVID-1984, I find myself in one of the strictest lock-downs in the world.

It might be slightly strange that under such circumstances I write a book about sovereignty and freedom, but here I am. And although right now is a time of increased government control, this crisis did reveal something: ever since this hysteria began, I haven't missed a beat. My income streams kept expanding. My assets remained untouched. Overall, I got ahead, while the world plunged into chaos. And as you'll discover, this isn't dumb luck but the result of careful planning...

Let's face it, all things you thought normal are off the table. This is the time for questioning your assumptions. How secure is everything around you? When the entire world can be taken hostage with the stroke of a pen, what can be done next? Now is the time to be defensive, agile, and protective. Keeping cool while everybody else goes crazy is vital. It is a time for relying on yourself and not the crumbling institutions around you. It is the time to become a *Crypto Sovereign*.

With this book, you instantly transform yourself into an expert on free and independent living. Learn the tactics the elite use to protect themselves and their wealth in times of turmoil. Understand the basics of paying taxes and when you're not required to pay anything at all. Discover the cleverest of tactics for asset protection. This book reveals a unique insight into how to structure your international affairs. If you're serious about being a sovereign crypto investor and living a life of ultimate freedom, *this book can change your life...*

But you'll have to make a choice:

...Keep reading to take full control of your journey; truly protect your assets and your wealth; break free from endless rules and regulations; stop being confused about legal and tax matters; become an independent and sovereign individual!

…Or close this book now to keep slaving away; living by someone else's rules; burdened by a life of uncertainty and dependence; feeling the snares of endless regulations suffocating you; putting your trust in the hands of people who don't have your interest at heart.

Decide now…

…Because after reading this book, there is <u>no</u> going back…

<Table of Contents_

1. < Introduction_   **1**

    1.1 What You Can Get From This Book   3

    1.2 Why I Wrote this Book   5

2. < Why Pay Taxes?_   **8**

    2.1 The Ways You're Squeezed   9

    2.2 Crypto-Currencies; Perfect for Tax Freedom   10

    2.3 The Eternal Welcome Guest   10

    2.4 Paying "Some" Taxes   12

3. < The KYC Crackdown_   **13**

    3.1 Money, Power, and Control   14

    3.2 Who Regulates Cryptos?   14

    3.3 Tax Evasion, Tax Avoidance   16

       3.3.1 The Google Analogy   16

    3.4 Tax Planning: Your Road to Freedom!   18

       3.4.1 Crystal Clear as a Mountain Stream   19

    3.5 Is this "Legal?"   20

4. < Why Everybody is Wrong about Cryptos_   **21**

    4.1 How are Bitcoins Taxed?   22

    4.2 "Bitcoins Cannot be Tracked"   23

5. < Powerful Legal Fundamentals_   **25**

    5.1 Is Justice Blind?   26

    5.2 The Other Side of the Shit-Coin   27

    5.3 Country vs State vs Tax Jurisdiction   27

    5.4 On-shore vs Off-shore   28

    5.5 The Hidden Secrets of Tax Law   29

       5.5.1 Taxing Rights   29

       5.5.2 Source of Income   30

       5.5.3 International vs Domestic   31

       5.5.4 Double Tax Treaties   31

5.6 Who Are You? Citizenship, Residence, Domicile   32

    5.6.1 Citizenship   32

    5.6.2 Residence   33

    5.6.3 Domicile   33

5.7 Ball & Chain: Tax Residence   34

    5.7.1 Fiscal Non-Residence   35

5.8 Different Income, Different Taxes   35

    5.8.1 The Common Goose Plucking   36

5.9 Long March to Freedom: the Tax Planning Funnel   38

5.10 Offshore Companies, Real or Utopia?   39

    5.10.1 Permanent Establishment Rules   40

    5.10.2 CFC Rules   41

    5.10.3 General Anti-Avoidance Rules   41

6.   < The Road to the Citadel_   43

6.1 Spread and Dissolve: International Diversification   44

6.2 The Elite's Closest Guarded Secret: Flag Theory   45

6.3 How Little You Need Might Surprise You   47

6.4 Join the International Fast-Lane   49

7.   < Residence – 1st Flag_   51

7.1 Different Tax Systems: Candy Shop for Grown-ups   51

    7.1.1 The Worldwide System   52

    7.1.2 The Territorial System   52

    7.1.3 Countries with No Income Tax   53

    7.1.4 Remittance Based System   54

    7.1.5 Citizenship-Based Taxation   54

    7.1.6 Special Programs Attracting High Caliber Hodlers   55

    7.1.7 Low Tax Countries   55

    7.1.8 The "We Don't Care" Model   55

7.2 Robust Tactics for Getting a New Residency   56

7.3 Staying on Tourist Visas   57

7.4 Moving within the EU   58

7.5 The Great Escape: Giving up Tax Residency   59

    7.5.1 Can You Keep Your House?   60

7.5.2 Center of Economic or Vital Interests 60

7.5.3 Tax Residency Scale 61

7.5.4 Bye Bye! What to do When Leaving 62

7.5.5 Emigrating With a Business or (Digital) Assets 63

7.5.6 Do You *Really* Have to Live There? 64

7.6 Always on Vacation 64

8.   < Business Base – 2nd Flag_ 66

8.1 What's Your Brilliance? 67

8.2 Bold New Income Streams 68

8.3 The Genesis Block of Business: the Corporation 69

8.4 How to Run a Corporation like a Pro 70

8.5 Corporation Stacking 71

8.6 Payday: How to Cash Out? 73

8.7 Selecting the Ideal Corporation 74

8.8 Tax Free Offshore Companies 76

8.9 Sole Proprietor... or Not? 77

9.   < Financial Services – 3rd Flag_ 79

9.1 Offshore Banking Decoded 80

9.1.1 FinTech Alternatives 81

9.2 Banking Secrecy 82

9.3 Financial Surveillance Shenanigans 82

9.4 Control Your Profile 84

9.5 How to Prevent Being Flagged as "Suspicious?" 85

9.6 Reasons for Opening Offshore Bank Accounts 87

9.7 Insider Tips for Opening Bank Accounts 88

9.8 What Do Banks Want? 90

9.8.1 Utility bill 90

9.8.2 Tax Residency Certificate 90

9.8.3 Source of Funds Report 91

9.8.4 Your Resume 91

9.8.5 Reference Letter 92

9.8.6 Passport Copy (of all the people involved) 92

9.8.7 Additional Requirements 93

9.8.8 Updated Bank Records 93

9.9 Taking Credit-Card Payments 94

9.10 Welcoming Crypto Payments 94

9.11 The Most Dangerous Number in Business 96

10. < Asset Haven – 4th Flag_ 97

10.1 Ploys of the Filthy Rich 97

10.2 The Mindset of the Global Wealth Builder 99

10.3 Next Level Hodling: International Assets 100

10.4 Keep Your Mouth SHUT! 101

10.5 Keep it Simple 103

10.6 Sovereign Investments 103

10.6.1 Impossible to Confiscate: Foreign Real Estate 104

10.6.2 Hard and Eternal: Precious Metals 104

10.6.3 Portable and Subtle: Intellectual Property 105

10.6.4 Skills, Reputation, Network, and Knowledge 106

10.7 Own Nothing, Control Everything 107

10.8 Building a Fortress against Scammers 109

10.8.1 The Long Term Con: Pyramid Schemes 110

10.8.2 The Houdini Act: High Yield Investment Schemes 110

10.8.3 How to Recognize Crypto-Currency Scams 111

11. < Playgrounds – 5th Flag_ 117

11.1 Work Hard, Play Hard 117

11.2 Living the Good Life 118

11.3 Settling Down in Paradise 118

12. < Citizenship – 6th Flag_ 121

12.1 Do You Need a Second Passport? 121

12.2 What is Citizenship? 123

12.3 Ways of Obtaining a Second Passport 124

12.4 Instant Nationality: Citizenship by Investment 125

12.5 The Citizenship Selection Process 125

12.6 The Power of Diplomatic and Unusual Passports 127

12.6.1 The Ultimate Insider's Club 128

12.7 Black Passports 129

13. < Cybersecurity – 7th Flag_   **130**

   13.1 Virtual Private Network (VPN)   131

   13.2 Sheltered Email Service   131

   13.3 Secure Data Storage   132

   13.4 Password Mastery   132

   13.5 Configure Your Computer for Privacy   132

   13.6 Secure Web-Hosting   133

   13.7 Planned Data Distribution   133

14. < Final Steps of Prudence_   **135**

   14.1 Health Insurance   135

   14.2 Don't Break the Law!   136

   14.3 Things that Suck About Being an Expat   138

   14.4 Don't Air Your Fiscal Laundry   139

   14.5 When in a Dispute with the (Tax) Authorities   140

15. < Americans (and Green Card Holders)_   **142**

   15.1 Filing Tax Returns   142

   15.2 Reporting of Accounts   143

   15.3 Tax Free Salary   144

   15.4 Tax Free Home   145

   15.5 Foreign Tax Credit   145

   15.6 Use of Corporations   146

<Afterword: The Road to True Liberty_   **147**

<Notes_   **151**

1. <Introduction_

My name is Wesley. For the last decade, I have been on the road to sovereignty. This is my journey. This is what I have learned. The tactics here provide a balanced account of how to achieve a life of real freedom, prosperity, and independence. I explored the ~~edges of legality~~ and learned to calmly walk the ~~middle of the road in a world trailing on the edge~~.

If you're invested in crypto currencies or interested in the space, this book propels you to the next level of understanding. The concepts in this book can transform you into a kick-ass, radically free, and truly fulfilled Crypto Sovereign. But before that, allow me to tell a bit about my background.

Living in Dubai, I got into Bitcoin in 2013. There was a lively community, with Bitcoin meet-ups and conferences. There were early fanatics convincing shops to accept Bitcoins, Arabs dreaming big of mining, and silent traders who since retired wealthy before the age of thirty. It was an exciting and new space!

It is hard to explain now, but it wasn't at all clear how cryptos would become valuable. It was still a community of geeks, cyberpunks, and radicals. I bought my first cryptos with the help of my landlord, who convinced me to buy Dogecoin. You had to first fund Paypal, and then use your balance to buy credits in a video game. These credits you exchanged for Bitcoin, which we exchanged for Doge on another site. We lost at least 35% in transaction fees; it felt like robbery and I did not want to buy more. But I figured there was a future because people were devoting themselves to the space full time, even back in 2013.

At the time, I was working at a firm that helped entrepreneurs and business owners move themselves and their business to Dubai. No taxes and few regulations were the main consideration. Sick and tired of being subjected to the growing pressure of the State, they "voted with their feet" to regain their economic freedom.

For myself, moving from a part of the world with the highest taxes in the world, to one without income taxes was eye-opening. Roads, schools, and hospitals were in great condition; crime and unemployment were nonexistent. The law protected privacy and property rights. The air buzzed with economic optimism and prosperity. Entrepreneurs and high-net-worth-individuals flocked there by the thousands. I helped them with the immigration process, opening bank accounts, and registering their businesses. By 2014, I installed a shopping card to start accepting Bitcoins, and we had a few clients paying with them.

I had a failed attempt at entrepreneurship myself even before moving to Dubai. And at the end of 2014, I decided to plunge into the deep again; I quit and moved to the Philippines, working on a small consulting business, capitalizing on what I learned about corporate structuring and international tax. A small section of my clients were Crypto Investors (**CI**s) and it was then that I received my first Bitcoin payments.

Due to the immaterial nature of crypto-currencies, investors can easily move to a country where they have to pay little or no taxes. Unfortunately, most CIs understood little of this, let alone know how to deal with international regulatory and financial systems. Funny enough, my consulting business closely followed the bull market; the higher Bitcoin rose, the more clients I had! After the crypto bubble popped by early 2018, so did this business.

By September 2017, it wasn't just money being decentralized; there were legal developments as well. Due to my background, I was highly interested. But upon closer inspection, none of the projects made any sense. There were Initial Coin Offerings pretending to be shares but not giving their buyers any rights; Smart Contracts that weren't contracts in the eyes of the law; Decentralized Arbitration that couldn't be enforced; and Decentralized Organizations that weren't organizations, nor decentralized.

I studied the white-papers of these projects, and compared them with actual textbooks on international law, arbitration, and legal philosophy. The main thing missing in all these projects was the legal framework, so I invented one based on open source development technologies. I published my findings in a white paper: *The Decentralized Legal System—the First Framework for Decentralized Law.*[1]

Besides focusing on cryptos, I dove deeper into international tax law. Together with a friend, I created a website on a specific type of tax law governing "transfer pricing." It now has the most visited blog on the topic in the world. I also published a text book on the subject in 2018, which I highly recommend if you ever have trouble sleeping. We also provide tax compliance services to medium sized international organizations and sell legal templates.

To summarize: I understand the legality of cryptos and how they relate to the laws governing our lives. Moreover, I have a deep understanding of international tax laws. As a result, I know exactly how laws apply to crypto investors and how to avoid them and regain sovereignty. What I learned is summarized in this book.

1.1 What You Can Get From This Book

This book differs from other books written about this topic. Other books are written by the rebel, for the rebel; they shun "real" information, and they tell you what can be done, but not how. These texts complain why we need more freedom using economic arguments or they tell you to "discuss it with your lawyer." Few books explain international taxation for individuals, let alone offer guidance on the taxes and (practical) reality of living as an international CI.

This book covers fundamentals. It explains enough of international regulations to help you get away from the bulk of it (if you wish). Nowadays, the rules are tightening and simple solutions don't work anymore. It's not an option to stay uninformed. I run into people who never look at laws and follow what "sounds" or "feels" best. Remember: you alone are responsible for your legal affairs. I help you understand fundamental concepts thereby reducing your dependence on advisors. I can tell you with authority that the majority of service agents, government employees, bankers, and yes, even tax professionals don't understand the concepts in this book.

Don't expect this book to address exactly your particular situation. Such advice depends on too many variables. This industry changes quickly. I want this book to be "timeless" and valuable ten years from now without having to update it every month because some law is updated. This is a book about principles not tactics.

This is also not an elaborate sales pitch. See it as a summary of a decade's journey to freedom. I tell it all in details. Moreover, I have included arguments from the most influential authors on the topic of international living. This treasure of information is not found anywhere else, and definitely not for this price.

As one of the few in this space, I do the grind-work of researching tax, international, crypto, and immigration law. As you'll see, I base the technical sections on textbooks and standards provided by leading organizations such as the EU, the OECD, and the UN. Feel free to follow up on the footnotes; they provide a wealth of information on how the world really works.

Currently, the most popular crypto-currency is Bitcoin. I think this will stay this way, but there is no guarantee. Regardless, the tactics in this book apply to all crypto-currencies. From now on, I will refer to them all as **crypto** (or **cryptos**).

This book starts with two introductory chapters. They're followed by three chapters: KYC, the legality of cryptos, and an explanation of crucial law and tax concepts. These chapters are explained as plainly as possible and give you unique and valuable insights found nowhere else—use this for the rest of your international (business) life. Next, I introduce flag theory, a concept used for decades by international elite to live life according to their own rules. The chapters that come after look at the different "flags" making up a successful international life, specifically focusing on investors in cryptos.

To summarize, I am going to explain how you can legally live a life of economic freedom. Eliminate paperwork, red tape, and bureaucratic hassles, and pay as little tax as possible (down to 0% on certain income streams). I explain what you can and can't do. These ideas are based on the principle of "voting with your feet." Moving to a place they treat you better. This isn't a guide on how to hide from the tax man—*those days are over*.

Unfortunately, voting with your feet alone does not work for Americans (or Green card holders). There are, however, ways Americans can benefit from the principles mentioned in this book. I have added a chapter with US tax planning tips at the end.

1.2   Why I Wrote this Book

First of all, I didn't plan on writing this book. I am neutral to its content. I used to be hardcore libertarian and opposed to taxes. Now, I am more of a "middle of the road" guy. If anything what I write here sounds radical, the problem is not me; society has drifted away from the mean. And I think this is becoming a problem.

What I propose is simple: a reasonable society. A low income tax and little government interference. The thing is, I am a student of history. And when others look at the past they are only interested in the highlights: the wars and revolutions. But if you look at the times of peace and prosperity, it was when people were largely left to themselves. You never find high taxes and endless regulation (or worldwide lock-downs) leading to a flourishing life. And thus, the current period is one of outliers. It will return to the mean—*as it always does*. This book gives you an early taste of what increased freedom feels like.

Governments and international organizations are becoming a serious problem for our liberty and peace of mind. Too many are educated in the art of wealth distribution as opposed to wealth creation. After their heads have been filled with collectivist propaganda and big dreams of changing the world, they join the army of middle managers at NGOs, intergovernmental organizations, and other parasitic institutions aimed at extracting more power and resources from the average person to combat whatever global "crisis" is invented next. Aristotle already explained this as a transition from democracy for the many to an oligarchy for the few. Because they are educated, rich, or powerful, they think they know how the rest of us should live. These transitions happen all the time.

My main goal is discussing this process and focus on Decentralized Law as an alternative. But so far, it has fallen on deaf ears. Now, I am taking a different angle. Let's admit, we crypto enthusiasts, besides having a healthy distrust of centralized control, are also a greedy bunch (refreshing Coinmarketcap forty times a day). So a book with tactics on escaping regulation and lowering taxes should land well.

But I do want to call your attention to the final chapter in this book, in which I am touching on the use of cryptos to regain liberty not just for you, but for the rest of the world. How to get back to life of individual dignity, with reigned in governments, and more peace of mind and prosperity. It used to be possible to move away from everything. But the tentacles of centralized power are increasingly strangling the globe. We might get to a point in the future when you cannot get away from invasive KYC, social credit-scores, and forced negative interest rates. Anyway, stick around until the final chapter.

On the main topic of this book, taxation, I myself have been on "both sides of the fence." I have advised people on how to pay as little taxes as possible by moving abroad. On the contrary, now the lion's share of my income comes from explaining people specific tax compliance rules. In a way, I am a glorified compliance officer myself. This is a funny realization because in an early draft of this book I joked that the world would be a better place if all compliance officers were tied down on a silk bed and tickled with large feathers.

Try to be neutral to the content of this book. It is just an explanation of how it is. Don't freak out or get emotional. There is logic and reason behind most legislation, and following logic and reason makes you a better person.

For the record, I am an advocate of liberty. I think that we need a global Magna Carta. We need to grab back our liberties and build our own systems away from these crumbling institutions. I have written some suggestions in the final chapter. But first, let me tell you what you can achieve before explaining what taxes are and how you get away from them.

The bottom line: you don't have to stay stuck in a town where you were accidentally born. It's a big world full of countries welcoming ambitious individuals. You can be yourself and build a life as extravagant or as reclusive as you want. Eliminate endless rules and regulation.

I hope reading this book helps you achieve an increased sense of freedom, independence, and sovereignty. Then, when your plans produce what you wanted, you can relax and enjoy. You can act spontaneously because you've eliminated bad consequences. Engulf yourself in a flow of genuine positive emotions and...

...taste all that life has to offer!

2.   <Why Pay Taxes?_

Western countries have been set up along a certain line: you pay a share of your income to the State, which in turn provides benefits such as a social security, health-care, education, and pensions. However, if you were to move away as a CI, you lose access to most, if not all of these benefits. You're no longer using the roads, the hospitals, or the schools. Paying for benefits to which you're not entitled doesn't make sense. Moreover, there is no legal obligation to do so.

A tax authority, bound by law, cannot tax at random. They need a legal basis for doing so. According to their own laws, a State does not have a right to tax you if you're a) not a resident, or b) don't generate income in that State. When you leave their jurisdiction, this legal basis disappears.

A resident of a State can choose to move to another one with extensive benefits, for example, moving from Germany to France. A new "Social Contract"[2] is established, and the new resident pays for the benefits enjoyed in the new country. As it turns out, other countries offer a contrasting system: no benefits, and nothing to pay!

In a nutshell, this is what this book is about: moving from a high-tax country to a low-tax one. There is nothing strange about this; even within the European Union, massive disparities exist between member States in terms of tax-rates and benefits. The freedom to choose between systems is one of the four fundamental "freedoms" of the EU,[3] albeit subjected to a few limitations and considerations[4]. Moreover, tax systems are firstly a domestic affair.[5] In short, the option of moving to a lower tax region will not disappear soon.

2.1 The Ways You're Squeezed

The Four Hour Work Week by Tim Ferris read like a call to arms for young adventurers. I encountered many others who moved to a new country after reading this book. In it, the concept of Geoarbitrage is defined: *"to exploit global pricing and currency differences for profit or lifestyle purposes."*[6] To sum it up: you move to a low cost country while you make your money in a high-tax one. The same income gets you much further, and your quality of life increases, too!

We can however add another dimension to this: living on a first world income, in a third world country, while lowering taxes. This is the concept of geotaxarbitrage:

> *To exploit global tax and regulatory differences for profit or lifestyle purposes.*

The next image demonstrates this:

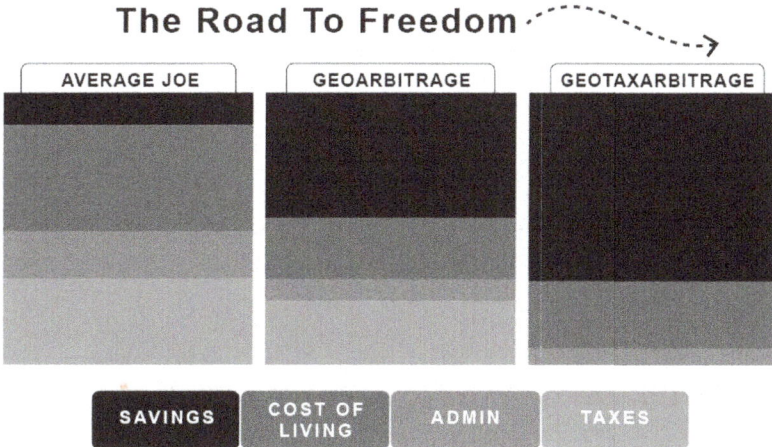

The Road To Freedom

| AVERAGE JOE | GEOARBITRAGE | GEOTAXARBITRAGE |

| SAVINGS | COST OF LIVING | ADMIN | TAXES |

Using this concept, you end up with a higher disposable income. And you see the "Admin & Reporting" section? In the high-tax world, you can have regulatory obligations such as filing extensive tax-returns, recording all your trades, or making difficult capital gains calculations. CIs need to hire help for this, which is an additional indirect cost that can be minimized with geotaxarbitrage.

Even with a cut in income, you might still come out ahead. You work less and gain more! You can start with little or nothing, yet end up comfortably wealthy. Once you start chopping away at the burden of taxes and regulations, you can focus on making money and doing what you are passionate about. When you spend little, you can save more. I have a friend, an older gentleman, who swears he is wealthy because he applied geotaxarbitrage early in life. Low-tax in combination with a long life equals prosperity!

2.2 Crypto-Currencies; Perfect for Tax Freedom

The world is flat. Technological progress connects the world. Move to the far side of the world and still be in touch with friends, family, clients, and employers (for better or worse). Businesses adapt. There's more remote work set up every day.

Readily available WIFI has made it possible for ambitious CIs to spread their wings while trading from a laptop. High-speed video calls and file sharing cost nothing. Precious information and educational material is readily available. Hodl in peace while checking your blockfolio from a white sandy beach while sipping a piña colada. It is even possible to run a business remotely!

One doesn't need to be a millionaire or have a large income to live an international life. Being ambitious, having a marketable skill-set, and a decent work ethic gets you a long way. Living can be cheap on the other side of the world, yet life is of a high quality.

Yes, being mobile and being able to live anywhere you want has a long list of benefits. One advantage, overlooked due to its perceived complexities, is the potential tax benefit. Everybody in high-tax countries can reduce taxation by moving. As you'll discover in this book, where you live is what matters most in taxation.

2.3 The Eternal Welcome Guest

A common misrepresentation seen in the media is that foreigners "exploit" countries when they aren't paying income taxes—especially when the countries are poor. This is a weird post-colonial welfare mentality, as if we're dealing with weak creatures incapable of independent thought. Taxation is a domestic affair, and these countries are free to decide their policies. They need investments, tourism, entrepreneurship, and job creators. They purposely welcome foreign capital by offering tax breaks.

Despite what the media, governments, and NGOs want you to believe, direct tax income is not the only economic benefit a foreign investor delivers. In areas popular with international entrepreneurs, the locals cannot build restaurants, co-working spaces, apartment buildings, and bars fast enough. This results in jobs, profits, and a higher standard of living.

Moreover, these economic gains don't deprive the host country of anything. Their pie grows. If a Vietnamese grows a coconut in his garden and sells it to a tourist for a few satoshis, Vietnam gained a few sathoshis in disposable income. This can be used to buy life's necessities such as medicine, selfie-sticks, and roosters for the fighting pit. All these satoshis add up.

Besides the economic benefits for the general public, (local) governments also benefit. Even when income isn't taxed, consumption is. Nearly all countries charge VAT or sales tax on purchases you make. There are tourist taxes on the use of hotels and airports. Gasoline and alcohol are taxed, as are tourist attractions and national parks. In addition, visa fees and elaborate financing schemes can be required in order to enter the country. And the economic activity CIs bring into the country results in profits and salaries for locals with taxation "down the line."

And let's not forget the long term effects. CIs are entrepreneurial types with unusual skills and positive attitudes. I have seen many who started out as tourists, establishing businesses and partnering up with the locals. They became productive upper-middle class residents, and influenced the local population in other beneficial ways by giving them ideas, coaching or employing them, and inspiring them with their ambition.

I strongly believe 10.000 CIs can turn any backwater, in ten years' time, into a prosperous city—even without paying a single dime in income taxes. CIs are, in a sense, superior versions of Robin Hood. Transferring honest hard capital from rich countries to poor ones! A desirable kind of tourist, respectful of local laws and authority, calm, low profile, and increasingly prosperous.

2.4 Paying "Some" Taxes

Not paying taxes can be counter-intuitive. International entrepreneurs regularly tell me they "feel" more comfortable by paying "some" taxes. I tell them that I read tax laws for a living and how they feel is never a consideration. Regardless, they prefer to register a corporation in Estonia as compared to sending an invoice in their own name from a tax-free residence. They end up paying taxes in countries they receive little benefits from; I am sure better charities can be found! And as you'll learn soon, when you pay taxes in a random place you still might not follow the law.

And let us not be too radical either. Realistically, taxes are a cost of doing business. It's not always possible to have 100% tax free income. There are plenty of cases where a low tax solution is the logical option. Better a taxed income, than no income at all! And certain types of income or residency situations simply cannot escape taxes either, as explained in a later section. Facts matter!

So remember, the goal is not to stop paying taxes, but to arrange your affairs efficiently. Should you give away your products and services for free to lower your tax bill? Of course not! You still want to sell as much as possible. I wish I paid millions in taxes. After all, if you pay a lot of taxes, this means you make a lot of money!

I hope this book allows you, dear reader, to make a calm, rational, and lawful decision as to how to arrange your affairs. To get to this stage, however, you first need to understand what can and cannot be done. This is discussed now...

3. <The KYC Crackdown_

I will never forget my first Bitcoin conference in Dubai. All excited, I went there with my boss and Brenda, a brilliant accountant. One speaker was an Argentinean compliance guy working in New York, who started his talk with how Bitcoin was going to "bank the unbanked" in Africa—*the familiar story*. But then he switched gears. He told us how Bitcoin shouldn't be allowed to remain unregulated. How the "laws were already in place" and we needed Bitcoin to be subjected to them. I couldn't believe what I was hearing! What's worse, the crowd handed him a strong applause because of his eloquent speaking.

Other than those visitors, I was overseeing the opening of bank accounts for my clients, and had witnessed firsthand the result of introducing strict KYC and AML laws in Dubai; the banks stopped taking on clients from Africa, who were deemed too risky, as well as those with small accounts, for whom the price of regulating them was too expensive. So much for banking the unbanked.

After the presentation we went for an explanation. Brenda was so angry she couldn't speak. I was up in his face about what he thought he was advocating for our beloved Bitcoin: our recently discovered frontier of liberty. He didn't have a clear defense, and stated that he is simply following the law. I couldn't stop arguing with him, and he started backpedaling. At one point, he shoved a business card in my hand, and when I looked at it he made a quick escape.

Perhaps I should have been friendlier, but we came for economic freedom and saw it slip through our fingers like Dubai's fine desert sand. It wasn't until two years later that the regulatory crackdown really picked up steam.

3.1   Money, Power, and Control

In 2016 the "Panama Papers"[7] made waves across the world. "Someone" leaked the administration of a company called Mossack Fonseca, exposing the characters behind offshore company structures. As it turned out, this was an insight on how the "elite" allegedly used offshore companies to hide their assets from tax authorities. Even a few politicians got caught in the net.[8]

It didn't take long for everybody with an ax to grind towards corporations and the "filthy" rich to start chiming in on how 32 trillion[9] US dollars' worth of assets existed in the "black hole" of offshore havens.

Look, offshore companies and banking secrecy are used to evade taxes. But the numbers thrown around are generally highly exaggerated[10] or simply fabricated![11]

Regardless, the media, politicians, and special interest groups invested heavily in the story and used it to start a war on financial privacy. Recent regulatory changes now monitor and control the financial system, reducing privacy and cutting off the financial system for everybody who is considered a "risk."

Despite the often touted money laundering and terrorist financing, it's mostly about taxes and control. This was confirmed to me by the head of compliance, who introduced KYC rules, at the central bank in Dubai. Maybe this was told to him in private, since money laundering and terrorist financing motivations were touted publicly. Exceedingly, nations are broke and want to close the exits. This affects you.

3.2   Who Regulates Cryptos?

Taxation is first and foremost a domestic affair. National governments determine what they tax and at what rate. An exception is the European Union, which is trying to create conformity within its member States. Value Added Taxes (VAT) are now harmonized in the EU for example, even though individual members States still determine the rates.

Besides the EU, other multinational organizations such as the UN, FATF, and OECD are creating rules to combat "harmful practices." Since no international constitution or legislative power exists, these organizations cannot create law. Instead, they create "standards" and "recommendations." These have to be accepted and implemented by individual governments before they can be considered law. In practice, all countries play ball. If not, they're placed on grey or black lists. This results in being cut off from the international financial system, spelling economic ruin—*an offer they can't refuse.*

This resulted in the strict KYC obligations for banks and other financial institutions. As you might have noticed, it was a piece of cake to include crypto exchanges and trading platforms under the same umbrella. CIs now face cumbersome and invasive procedures when they want to buy or sell cryptos. Moreover, information on accounts is exchanged with the country of residence of the account holder. This eliminates financial secrecy and easy ways to hide from the tax man. But what is worrying, is it gives strong control to what is and isn't allowed.

To summarize: intergovernmental organizations stirred up the Panama Paper commotion by highly exacerbating the problem, arguing a global solution is needed, and then offering the solution. They obtained a grip over the financial service providers, including those where cryptos are traded. This is the reason why every exchange around the world has similar requirements. This is not because of your government, but because a group of international faceless bureaucrats you haven't voted for and have no power to remove.

So remember this the next time you see a post on r/bitcoin that if only a fraction of the money that is "hidden offshore" is invested into Bitcoin, it will moon. Or when someone complains that governments are too strict with KYC, and they should do something about the Panama Papers and banks instead.[12] KYC regulations are what "they" did.

On a more optimistic note, let us not forget that these regulations apply to service providers; they still date from the mindset that banks facilitate transactions. The major difference with the traditional financial system and cryptos is that with cryptos you don't need a third-party for transactions. You can send cryptos yourself directly to whomever you want. And no one can stop you from downloading an app and receiving payments from all over the world for next to nothing in transaction costs. This is powerful. Once peer-to-peer transactions pick up, the ability to control and monitor is drastically reduced. In addition, there are still many legal methods to lowering regulatory and tax burdens by moving across borders—*since tax rates haven't changed*. But before we can understand what is possible, we first have to understand what isn't.

3.3 Tax Evasion, Tax Avoidance

During the ongoing regulatory crackdown "Tax Evasion" and "Tax Avoidance" are often lumped together. This doesn't seem fair. Tax evasion consists of willing illegal behavior, such as sending fake invoices. With tax avoidance, you use international law instruments, such as tax treaties, to lower taxes. Because it's difficult to explain why those following the law are now scrutinized, here's an analogy.

3.3.1 The Google Analogy

Google allows you to type in a keyword and search the web for relevant pages. Since many searches are being done through Google, ranking highly is critical for (online) businesses. A brand new discipline emerged: Search Engine Optimization (SEO).

> In the earliest days of SEO, it was relatively easy to "game" the system. You didn't need high quality content: a page stuffed with keywords ended high up in the search rankings. The content could be garbage, and Google did not like this. Over time, they got more sophisticated. Third-party validation became important, and if other websites linked to a page it helped with the rankings. It didn't take long for "SEOs" to start adding links from the strangest corners of the Internet. Websites without real content offered links for sale. This worked for a while, and then Google wizened up again. It dropped the value of links from poor sites, and even

penalized sites with shoddy incoming links. Google now looks at a flood of new metrics. It has gotten difficult to game the system. The bottom line is that Google wants articles with substance, to ensure their readers receive valuable content. As long as you create quality content, you're never penalized.

How does this relate to our discussion on taxation? Well, back in the day, many "black hat" options for not paying taxes were available. It was easy to open a bank account in a country with banking secrecy or receive a tax-free income stream in an offshore company. When governments got fed up with this and focused on banking transparency, the use of holding companies became common. These holding companies made use of tax treaties, but nothing happened in the country of registration. The latest rounds of regulatory measurements have restricted this practice. The argument boils down to... substance. Are substantial activities happening in the country the profits are "taxed?" *Sound familiar?*

With this in mind, we can go back to our definitions. Things used to be simple: Tax evasion is illegal while tax avoidance is legal. But now tax avoidance is considered harmful by a growing group of regulators, especially when it involves bending the rules too aggressively. Tax avoidance is of concern because such practices *"contrary to fiscal equity, have serious budgetary effects and distort international competition and capital flows."*[13] In addition, according to the OECD, tax avoidance contains elements of secrecy, artificiality, and using provisions in ways for which they weren't intended.[14]

Given the freedom private persons have in arranging their affairs, a wide variety of tactics can be applied to lowering taxes. Besides avoidance and evasion, there is one other category: tax planning, the lowering of taxes in full accordance with the law. It would be best to have a clear definition of when behavior is considered harmful and when not. Sadly, no clear distinction exists between tax avoidance and tax planning.[15]

For simplicity, in the remainder of this book, the word evading means breaking the law, and "avoiding" means avoiding taxes by legal and acceptable tax planning.

Tax payers' behaviors are generally categorized as "aggressive" if their only aim is to lower taxes. Highly aggressive behaviors might be labeled as "harmful tax avoidance" and result in audits. If we go back to the Google Analogy, evasion, avoidance, and planning would be Black Hat, Grey Hat, and White Hat tactics respectively. The below image demonstrates the three categories. A diagram measures the level of "good" and "bad" behavior of a tax payers. Behavior categorized as too aggressive might result in unacceptable tax avoidance.

3.4 Tax Planning: Your Road to Freedom!

Luckily, we have tax planning: a truly legal type of tax lowering behavior. In some cases, it's expected! If, for example, a company can hire foreign consultant A for 200 USD per hour, and consultant B for 200 USD + 25% VAT, it logically prefers consultant A to avoid paying and addition 25% in VAT.

This type of legal tax minimization, over time, has been condoned by judges around the world. For example in the UK, Lord Tomlin Stated: *"Every man is entitled, if he can, to order his affairs so that the tax attaching under the appropriate Acts is less than it otherwise would be."* In Australia Stark J. wrote: *"There is nothing wrong in companies and shareholders entering, if they can, into transactions for the purpose of avoiding, or relieving them of taxation (...)."* And in the US Judge Learned Hand of the Supreme Court stated: *"Any one may so arrange his affairs that his taxes shall be as low as possible; he is not bound to choose that pattern which will best pay the Treasury; there is not even a patriotic duty to increase one's taxes."*[16]

For this book, we look at altering economic activity in order to benefit from a lower tax rate. This is known as substantive tax planning. These can be the transfer of a tax subject, the transfer of a tax object, or both.[17] For CIs, the following are acceptable forms of tax planning:

1. Moving yourself (subject) to a low-tax country
2. Starting a business (object) in a low tax country
3. Both

The migration of a CI, by changing tax residence, is an acceptable form of tax planning. Investing in foreign business is also perfectly okay. How to do this is explained in later chapters.

3.4.1 Crystal Clear as a Mountain Stream

We now know what can and cannot be done. The cards are on the table. Regardless of the provisions to combat artificial arrangements, taxation is still a national affair. And the way countries tax hardly changes; this would eliminate centuries of precedence, and create tremendous legal uncertainty for businesses. Moreover, domestic tax rates rarely change over time, and if they do, slowly.

Little can be done to those moving away, both legally and morally. If you're sick of high taxes in northern Europe, no one can stop you from moving to Bulgaria, with a 10% flat income tax. A government restricting this would face the full force of the European Union. With the Marrakesh Pact, the UN has tried to "regulate" the orderly migration into Europe by attributing all sorts of rights and benefits to migrants.[18] But if migrants can flock to Western Europe and use the welfare system without citizenship or ever paying taxes, no one—*legally nor morally*—can be stopped from moving away and not using it.

19

3.5　Is this "Legal?"

Sometimes I sense fear in CIs when discussing low taxes, as if it's illegal and outrageous. But it goes deeper. They experience an eerie suspicion and feel that their every move is being watched by the eye of Sauron. Scared little bunnies, hiding in the grass, afraid of the soaring eagle above.

This sentiment isn't entirely unjustified. The American IRS has been known for zero tolerance towards tax evaders, and a client told me that Australian tax inspectors have targets (KPIs) for the amount of serfs they send to jail. Convicting a high level person for a tax crime could benefit a civil servant's career, and I (indirectly) heard from a person high-up within the Dutch tax authorities that they pursue high profile cases for "scaring" the general public into compliance, appearing more powerful than they are.

Governments have limited time and resources and little incentive for going after law abiding citizens. If you read actual court cases, the problems mostly have to do with those having unclear residency situations (and still factually living in a high tax country), artificial business structures, and fraud. Sometimes, accusations are used to "cancel" people with the wrong political beliefs. However, I have never seen anybody getting into trouble for immigration itself. Mobile persons can reduce or eliminate taxes and remain lawful and transparent while doing so!

No tax law could be written (short of 100% confiscation) without ways around it. As one loophole closes, another opens up. If you want to cut your taxes, you can do it. But before we dive into these elite tactics, we first need to look at what everybody in the crypto-space is wrong about. What I am about to tell you goes against common knowledge, but it is essential if you don't want to trap yourself.

4.   <Why Everybody is Wrong about Cryptos_

We saw that governments simply designated exchanges as financial services providers. In one swoop, the entire industry was brought into the fold. What was originally considered an anonymous currency for radicals, turned out to be traceable by law enforcement with all entry and exit points tightly regulated and monitored. This miscalculation of how cryptos would work in the real world isn't restricted to Bitcoin payments.

Ever since the Ethereum white-paper was published,[19] the crypto world fantasized about decentralizing everything: from tokenizing real estate, and replacing insurance companies with smart contracts, to setting up legal entities in cyberspace. Without exception, these projects focus on technological possibility, not on legal reality.

Existing legal systems are based on ideas and best practices dating back thousands of years. They are subject to changing opinions and ideologies. Their definitions are debated and their outcomes uncertain. Decentralized technologies on the other hand, are based on hard sciences such as mathematics and cryptography. These systems are both transparent and open source, and they result in predictable outcomes. This discrepancy cannot be fixed by technological developments alone.[20]

Smart contracts on their own aren't legally binding. Decentralized Autonomous Organizations (DAOs) aren't legal persons before the law and cannot own anything. Decentralized arbitration cannot be enforced in the real world. It can be quite surprising, especially when you realize that many of these projects raised millions during the ICO craze. Even today, the CEO of the largest crypto exchange argues they are outside the legal system because their project is "decentralized."[21]

Another example: tokenization. In our current legal system, only a "person" owns assets. If you want to divide the ownership of an asset and make it easily transferable, you have to tokenize the person, not the asset. It is unlikely, that current land or business registers would be excited about tracking thousands of instantly transferable ownership details; or processing a transfer requiring one thousand signatories, half of which lost their password. The only real solution would be to create a fictive person before the law of which the ownership is easily transferable. Guess what? This already exists: a corporation.

Nearly all of these projects require a legal framework or changes in the legal system. This is a legal and often a political process, but it's not a technical one. This is never mentioned in any white papers. I could go into more depth, but the main conclusion for now is that we must ignore common ideas in the crypto-space and stick with existing legal principles.

4.1   How are Bitcoins Taxed?

We saw that one key fault with CIs is ignoring the concept of personality. And personality also matters in tax. After all you, as a person, are taxed based on your income and the assets you own. Without arrangements, all your activity in the crypto space is attributed to... you!

It also means that you aren't protected by limited liability in your activities. It is as if everything you do in the decentralized world, you do as a sole trader. And doing business as a sole trader opens you up to unlimited liability and generally the highest tax bills.

What does this mean in practice? For example, if you're paid for services in Bitcoin, this is personal income. If you make a profit during a trade, this is a personal gain. If you earn a return from staking in decentralized finance, this is personal income as well. Any time you transfer Bitcoins, this could be a taxable event. How this is taxed depends on where you, the person, live. As it turns out, there are countries without income taxes, or income taxes on certain transactions. The next chapters explain this.

And don't freak out just yet! There are great things about cryptos. For example, they do allow for radical control over your funds. They allow you to become much better at defending your property rights, shield yourself from out of control regulation, and live more privately.

As mentioned, if you want to cut your taxes, you can. But before we dive into these radical tactics, we first need to define essential aspects of international (tax) law. I advise to read it carefully. Although these concepts are simple, few understand them. Prepare to be enlightened...

4.2 "Bitcoins Cannot be Tracked"

I often see comments of people who think because Bitcoin is semi-anonymous transactions can be kept out of sight of the government. They either worry that governments cannot collect enough or dream of keeping their earnings secret.

This line of thinking misses something nontrivial: history. Up until fairly recently payments were done with cash and governments could not track these either. Yet, taxes have been charged and paid for centuries. Again, let us not forget that persons are taxed and persons can be audited. Most people have jobs, mortgages and insurance contracts. Their financial lives aren't particularly secret. The records of many corporations are public as well.

Furthermore, blockchains are *public* ledgers. This means that transactions can be scrutinized by anyone with time and resources. Whenever both transaction partners are unknown, transactions are indeed anonymous. But the moment one of the parties is known itself, the blockchain becomes a Sudoku puzzle potentially revealing all your transactions. Blockchain payment systems are bad for crime. Moreover, I have already seen trial balloons sent up on using mandatory assigned addresses and smart contracts that automatically pay a percentage in sales tax to the government. Those relying on blockchain secrecy might experience the same as those who relied on banking secrecy—*all works well, until one day it doesn't...*

5. <Powerful Legal Fundamentals_

Crypto enthusiasts are binary people; they think in ones and zeros. As a result, they interpret tax laws like speed laws: you either drive within the speed limits, or too fast. The reality is different. It's as if each road has a police officer with his own ideas of what speeding is; certain police officers don't enforce speeding laws, and on set roads you can legally drive as fast as you want. Some find this lack of certainty annoying but an optimist sees the opportunity!

Fiscal affairs, just as finances, career choices, and your love life cannot be fully outsourced. You don't have to understand everything 100%. But you need a general idea of what's going on. I have seen quite a few "babes lost in the woods." You alone are responsible, don't forget that!

At first, I'll discuss a few overall concepts which helped me understand the workings of tax and legal systems. Then I'll explain a few important principles underlying international taxation in a plain and concise manner, without a specific country in mind.

If you understand this now, it can benefit you for the rest of your (tax-free) life. On the other hand, if you have difficulties understanding the concepts, please stick to simple structures for the rest of your life. Pursuing strategies you don't understand is asking for trouble.

5.1 Is Justice Blind?

I have a friend who is an immigration lawyer on behalf of the government. His office accepts or rejects asylum applications from "refugees." Whenever a decision is made, applicants can appeal. I visited one of these court sessions.

One case concerned an epileptic Syrian. He had fled to Greece, where they registered him as an asylum seeker. According to him, the medication he needed wasn't available, and he soon found himself having seizures on the streets of Athens. He moved to the Netherlands where he was housed and medicated. Naturally, he wanted to stay. Yet, EU law dictates that refugees process their asylum in the country they first register. "Asylum shopping" is not allowed. It was determined that Greece was a safe place to return, and the medication was in fact available. His appeal was denied.

This story highlights a critical aspect of the justice system. Greece is in crisis. Medication is not readily available, not even for the local population. Who knows where this man will end up? But as my friend told me, if this was allowed now, a flood of refugees would start moving through Europe, clogging the systems with half-finished cases and putting pressure on facilities. It would remove the last hope of orderly migration into Europe.

Moreover, even though to me this case sounded believable, migrants lie all the time. When a report came out on oppression of a certain tribe in Somalia, soon more "members" of this tribe requested asylum in Europe than ever existed. Dealing with lies everyday makes you indifferent. My friend only wanted the judge to confirm the EU's practice, which she did.

The government approaches things objectively and impersonally. A case can be a test to create clarity on a new law or to sharpen a department's policy. If you're on the other side of the fence, the results of such a system might not always feel like true justice. Stay away from confrontations with the State and don't assume you're fine when innocent. The justice system is indeed blind, and ultimately it's not there to protect you: it protects "society."

5.2   The Other Side of the Shit-Coin

Another friend of mine worked at an elite tax law firm. A client of theirs wanted to deduct certain business costs as expenses. The tax authorities made a statement that those costs could not be deducted. But according to the law, deducting costs is an integral part of taxation—*they are two sides of the same coin*. The firm's position was that if the deduction of costs wasn't allowed, than neither was taxation. The judge went along with it. The company ended up paying nothing, and the tax authorities became more careful.

Large companies succeed better in treating the government as equals; individuals again and again curl up into a shivering little ball the moment the authorities come on the scene. Understandably, of course, but worth remembering.

Legal systems in the Western world depend highly on logic. There are two sides to each policy or ruling. When something is specifically restricted, something else is confirmed possible. For example, when artificial tax avoidance is restricted, non-artificial tax planning isn't. This kind of logic is applied throughout this book.

5.3   Country vs State vs Tax Jurisdiction

There have been a number of projects in the crypto-space trying to come up with their own countries and jurisdictions. These appear to be mostly people getting together complaining that the government sucks. As of now, I haven't come across a serious alternative to existing jurisdictions. There is one alternative, and that is the Consensus Jurisdiction. Here, participants voluntarily accept a set of binding rules to govern themselves by using a decentralized network.[22] For now, we stick to traditional definitions.

The State

A State, according to the widely accepted 1933 Montevideo Convention, is defined as:

...a person of International Law who possesses the following qualifications:

a) *a permanent population*

b) *a defined territory*

c) *a government*

d) *the capacity to enter into relations with the other States.*[23]

Jurisdiction

In the legal world, often the term jurisdiction is used. It's not the same as State. *"Jurisdiction is the term that describes the limits of the legal competence of a State or other regulatory authority to make, apply, and enforce rules of conduct upon persons."*[24] It describes the practical authority to deal with and enforce legal matters, one of which is the application of tax laws. Logically, it is the State that through its government has the power to enforce its taxing rights on the permanent population in a defined territory.

Central governments delegate taxing rights to local governments on the regional and municipality level as well. Think for example about property taxes or contributions to garbage collection. As a result, moving from one city to another within the same country can already lower your tax bill.

States can also consist of multiple tax jurisdictions with distinct income tax rates. Examples are the Cantons making up Switzerland, special administrative areas in Malaysia, and the states in the US. You can move yourself, or your business to other jurisdictions. As a result, this industry typically talks about jurisdictions rather than countries or States.

For simplicity reasons, in the remainder of this book the words country and State (capitalized) are used synonymously.

5.4   On-shore vs Off-shore

In this book, you'll encounter words such as offshore company and offshore bank account. What are they? I did an "Offshore Finance" course from an old Swiss banker while in Dubai. He defined a company or bank account as offshore when registered in a country outside of a subject's residency. When a person lives in Belgium and has a bank account in France, it's an offshore bank account. Not so scary, right? I've seen this definition repeated in old school sources.

For completeness, there are specific types of legal entities, typically registered in small tropical islands. These are exempt from taxation and reporting requirements, as long as they do business *outside* the jurisdiction of registration.[25] These types of legal entities are also often described as offshore companies.

For simplicity, in this book, when we talk about offshore, we stick to the following: a registration outside your State of residence.

5.5   The Hidden Secrets of Tax Law

For productive individuals living in the Western world, taxes may seem excessive and unfair. However, their enforcement follows a logic; the same laws forcing you to pay and restrict the authorities in what they can tax. States have what are called "taxing rights," or the "right to levy." The moment you understand where this right starts and ends, you can play with it.

5.5.1 Taxing Rights

In general, the right of a State to tax is based on two principles:[26]

1. A connection of a person with the jurisdiction (such as residence, incorporation or permanent establishment). This is known as "Residence Jurisdiction" (more below).
2. A source of income within the jurisdiction. This is known as "Source Jurisdiction."

A tax system must define when a person is a resident in its territory for tax purposes and when income is sourced in its territory. If you (or your income) don't fall within this definition, a State does <u>not</u> have the right to tax you.

5.5.2 Source of Income

The historical basis for the currently applied criteria for source jurisdiction (of income) can be found in a report written by four economists in 1923 at the request of the League of Nations (predecessor to the UN). It concludes that tax jurisdiction should be based on "economic allegiance," which consists of four aspects: origin, situs, legal status, and domicile.[27]

Diving into each demands too much detail. To summarize; both legality (e.g. how a business is structured) and economic reality (e.g. how a business is run) play a part when determining source of income.

I found a clarifying interpretation of a US Supreme Court Ruling on sourcing of income. It was made by the Supreme Court of the Philippines, which inherited the tax system of the US due to its colonial past.

> *The Supreme Court has said, in a definition much quoted but often debated, that income may be derived from three possible sources only: (1)* **capital** *and/or (2)* **labor;** *and/or (3)* **the sale of capital assets.** *While the three elements of this attempt at definition need not be accepted as all-inclusive, they serve as useful guides in any inquiry into whether a particular item is from "sources within the United States" and suggest an investigation into the nature and location of the activities or property which produce the income.*
>
> **If the income is from labor the place where the labor is done should be decisive**; *if it is done in this country, the income should be from "sources within the United States."* **If the income is from capital, the place where the capital is employed should be decisive**; *if it is employed in this country, the income should be from "sources within the United States."* **If the income is from the sale of capital assets, the place where the sale is made should be likewise decisive.**[28]

In short, the location where economic activity takes place matters. Keep in mind, though, that this is one interpretation made by one court in one country at one moment in time. As mentioned, this interpretation is debated by scholars and legislators alike.

It is crucial to know that there are countries with a divergent approach, and in practice employ a basic test: do you work for local customers. In such countries, they care little about what you do on your laptop if it doesn't involve their jurisdiction.

Every case is unique. Every interpretation is different. There are fifty shades of white and grey before you get to black. And there are non-stop disputes around the world over the application of this concept. Remember this next time someone posts that trading on a laptop without a visa is "100% illegal." Or making the common error of using their particular experience as the standard to all things.

5.5.3   International vs Domestic

Tax is strictly levied by individual States; domestic laws determine tax liability. International organizations don't have taxing rights, and no international tax laws exist in the traditional sense. Instead, the term "international tax law" indicates a set of rules affecting the tax treatment of cross-border operations. This set of rules is constituted, again, primarily by domestic tax rules, whose application is generally limited by double tax treaties, and other international law instruments.[29]

The OECD and EU do create extensive standards on tax matters. However, they must be entered into domestic legislation by individual States before they have force. And States don't always do this with the same conviction, or they apply variations. In order to understand your possible tax obligations, domestic legislation is <u>always</u> the first place to look.

5.5.4   Double Tax Treaties

Domestic taxing rules have varying definitions of residence and source of income. As a result, a person risks being considered a tax resident in two countries and having the same income taxed twice. To prevent this, cooperating States sign double tax treaties with one another. The goal of these treaties is to provide clarity for tax payers, and thus stimulate economic activities without tax risk.

Double tax treaties are a familiar example of international tax laws. They fit the definition mentioned above perfectly, considering tax treaties don't create taxing rights for a State.[30] Instead, *they create rights for a tax payer*, preventing them from being taxed twice on the same income. You can never be obliged to pay taxes based on a tax treaty. In fact, tax treaties are based on standard templates, and they can contain tax rates for taxes you're not even obliged to pay! For example, the tax treaty between Canada and the UK state that dividend paid from the UK to a shareholder in Canada may be taxed in the UK at 15%. But the UK doesn't tax outgoing dividends, so the real tax is 0%.[31]

It can be argued that for most Cis, tax treaties aren't too relevant; in order to apply one, <u>economic reality</u> needs to be taken in account. A CI living in Europe and trading from a laptop can hardly prove economic activity took place in a corporation in the British Virgin Islands. Certain CIs, however, can have other foreign sourced (passive) income. Examples are those investing in foreign companies or assets, receiving affiliate income from websites or royalty income from a book, or advertising income from a YouTube channel.

5.6 Who Are You? Citizenship, Residence, Domicile

Cis regularly confuse the concepts of citizenship and residence. If you want to take the international living fast-lane, I can't think of more fundamental knowledge. From a tax perspective, residence is essential, and citizenship matters only in highly specific cases (and for US citizens). Adding to the complexity, other concepts influence tax obligations, such as domicile, tax residence, and tax non-residence. Let's explore each.

5.6.1 Citizenship

You are a citizen of the country you have a passport from. All citizens of a country have the same rights, privileges, and duties as defined by law. A citizen of a country can expect protection from the State he is a citizen of, and have the right to move freely in the country. In return, a citizen might be liable for civil duties or military service. Individuals can hold multiple citizenships, although not all countries allow it. More on citizenship later.

5.6.2 Residence

Legal residency constitutes your right to live, work, or study in a country. A residence permit is issued, which is often time-limited and comes with certain obligations to keep the residency valid. Examples are a minimum number of days you have to stay in the country, investing a certain amount, having a job, or running a business. Such restrictions don't apply when you're a citizen.

You keep your existing citizenship (passport) when you become a resident in a new country. Most countries allow you to become a citizen after a few years of residence, but this is not mandatory. The process of getting residence in a tax-friendly country is discussed in later chapters.

5.6.3 Domicile

Domicile is a vague and misunderstood concept, and from a tax perspective mostly relevant in common law systems. Common law is practiced in the UK and its former colonies. According to the HRMC, *"domicile is the criterion adopted by the common law for connecting the individual, either directly or indirectly through dependence on another individual, to a system of municipal law."*[32] Generally, a domicile is assigned by birth, but changing your domicile is possible. This is not as easy as changing residence, but more like adopting a new home-country. One can only have one domicile at a time.

Various States establish taxing rights based on domicile. In the UK, domicile matters for inheritance taxes, and Ireland has a "domicile levy" for wealthy individuals, even if the subject is not a resident.[33] Australia included domicile in their definition of tax residency, meaning an Australian is always a tax resident until he changes his domicile.[34]

As always, the domicile concept can be reversed to your benefit. The UK (and many of its former overseas territories such as Barbados and Malta) have arrangements for non-domiciled residents who receive income from offshore sources in a bank account outside the UK. Income remitted in such a way is exempt from taxes. Now you know how wealthy Russians and Arabs live princely in London (as long as they aren't crashing their Lambos).

5.7   Ball & Chain: Tax Residence

Changes in residence and domicile are a matter of personal intention, not a matter of physical presence. For example, an Irish oil worker moves to Sri Lanka to start a family and build a life. His residence and domicile changes. The logical conclusion? He now has to pay taxes in Sri Lanka. But as it turns out, he spends eight months of the year in Indonesia working on an oil rig. Consequently, he finds himself above the 183 day threshold in Indonesia, and has to pay tax there.[35] He doesn't have to pay taxes in Sri Lanka, as he stays there under 183 days.[36]

When owning a business in Dubai, you can apply for a visa. You only need to visit one time in each 180 days for this visa to remain valid. Some CIs think this is all they have to do to become a "resident" in Dubai (no income taxes). However, this ship doesn't always sail; from a fiscal perspective, facts matter. Even if one has legal residence, this doesn't say anything about where he factually resides. After all, a CI can secure residence permits in two or more countries!

To establish taxing rights, States have criteria determining if one is a "resident for tax purposes." A common example is the 183 rule: when you stay more than 183 days, you're liable for taxes. But the 183 day is not holy: In Hong Kong, it takes 60 days to be liable for taxes[37] (albeit only on local sourced income). In the UK, it's only 16 days if you've recently been a previous tax payer. In France, having a house or business alone can satisfy the criteria.[38] My country of birth, the Netherlands, determines taxing rights based on "circumstances,"[39] a vague and expanding definition which often leads to disputes.

No single definition determines tax residency, and facts matter. This is why banks always ask for proof of where you live—such as a utility bill. To repeat, a residence permit allows you to stay somewhere; it doesn't prove you do. Tax residence is all about facts.

5.7.1 Fiscal Non-Residence

By now you've picked up the correct logic and ask yourself: what if I don't meet any requirements for tax residence? What if I stay under 60 days in Hong Kong, under 183 days in Sri Lanka and don't own a house or a business in France? Well, my smart reader, then you're not obliged to pay taxes in these countries!

This concept is known as being tax non-resident, and more commonly, a PT. We explore this topic in later chapters.

5.8 Different Income, Different Taxes

Debates on tax mostly revolve around personal income tax. Most people have jobs, after all. However, there are other types of income, and thus other types of taxes. A CI can have multiple income streams that are all taxed differently. Examples of this are dividend income from an investment in Europe, royalty income from Amazon, and local salary in the country of residence. And you guessed it, this opens ways to plan.

The distinction is often made between passive and active income. Active income comes from hourly work such as consultancy, freelancing, and remote jobs. Examples of passive income are profits from investments and royalties. As we saw, the main question in the taxation of income is the question of "source." As a rule of thumb, active income is taxed where activities are performed, and passive income is taxed where the assets are exploited. Exceptions exist, of course.

It is worth noting that even high-tax countries approach taxation in a variety of ways. Canada, the UK, and Australia tax capital gains on cryptos. In the Netherlands, crypto investments are considered income from savings and investments (Box III).[40] There isn't a capital gains tax. Instead, on 1 January of every tax year you need to summarize how much your coins are worth and pay a small "wealth tax" (regardless of gains or loses made). This tax is due every year as long as you own this wealth, which strikes foreigners as bizarre.

What to do? First, realize gains in countries without capital gains tax. Next, move to a country without wealth tax!

5.8.1 The Common Goose Plucking

Governments, over time, have taxed all but breathing and sitting in the sun (and even of that I am not certain). It was Jean-Baptiste Colbert, the French economic assistant to Louis XIV who said *"the art of taxation, consists in so plucking the goose as to obtain the largest amount of feathers with the least amount of hissing."*[41]

These are the common feathers plucked:

- **Personal Income Tax**. The most common way to make money is by having a job. Income taxes take a big chunk. This type of tax is often levied on a progressive scale, with higher incomes paying a higher percentage of tax. In the Western world, income in the top brackets is taxed to over 50%. Sole traders are taxed similarly, although they usually benefit from incentives to stimulate entrepreneurship, such as a tax-free allowance and the ability to deduct business expenses. Keep in mind that you are the legal person owning the cryptos, and thus any income for work paid to you in cryptos could be consider personal income—including income generated by novel means, such as staking, mining, running a node, or DeFi.

- **Dividend tax**. This is a tax levied on profit distributions paid by a corporation to its shareholders. This tax is often less than income tax, but corporations first pay tax on their income, and dividend tax comes next. There are however States where corporations aren't taxed on income, on outgoing dividends, or both. There are crypto-projects paying dividends to those holding tokens, but just because it is called a dividend doesn't mean it is one.

- **Capital Gains Tax**. If you invest in an asset and sell it at a profit, you realize a capital gain. Capital gains tax is levied on this profit. Examples are gains realized from the sale of stocks, bonds, real estate—*and of course cryptos*. On the flip-side, capital losses create a tax-credit. Capital gains tax is not levied everywhere, or for example only on real estate. There are countries without capital gains tax or without capital gains tax for cryptos (and the reporting coming with it).

- **Royalties Tax**. Royalties are license fees for intellectual property, such as patents, books, websites, or brands. Royalty income is usually taxed at source, but not always. In the past, this has resulted in lowering of the tax bills of companies in high tax jurisdictions by invoicing for intellectual property such as brands (Nike) and coffee recipes (Starbucks). This caused a lot of controversy. I have never seen any small business successfully using these tactics. Royalty tax does apply to several small business income streams, such as Amazon book sales. This royalty income is taxed at source in the US at 30%, unless a tax treaty can be applied.[42] The trick is to go through the list of treaties and look for a country with residence based taxation (no tax on foreign sourced income).

- **Value added taxes (VAT) / Sales Tax**. This somewhat hidden tax can be a State's biggest source of income, given that it's levied on (almost) everything bought and sold. While the earlier taxes were a tax on income, this is a tax on consumption. Let's not forget, these are taxes you pay when spending income on which you *already paid* income taxes. There are countries without VAT, such as the US (at least on the federal level), and Hong Kong. The EU, on the other hand, has introduced VAT on digital products which even applies to businesses not in the EU.[43] For freelancers selling to the other side of the world, VAT is a hard cost. Eliminating VAT allows them to price more competitively, or earn up to 25% (Denmark) extra income. One crypto activity commonly attracting VAT is mining. Likewise, other business activities such as selling digital products to the EU.

- **Wealth tax.** A wealth tax is a tax on the total value of personal assets. This can include cash, bank deposits, investment real estate, stocks, bonds, and digital assets. Typically, liabilities (primarily mortgages and other loans) can be deducted, hence it's sometimes called a net wealth tax. Few countries have a wealth tax; examples are the Netherlands and Argentina.

- **Real Estate**. I have met CIs who cashed in cryptos and moved to rental income. Such income is usually taxed where the property is located. Other kinds of property taxes, such as transfer tax, or municipality tax, can also apply. Little tax planning is possible with real estate, since it's pretty obvious where the taxable object is. One can buy investment property in countries where rental income and capital gains aren't taxed (Dubai), or taxed minimally (the Dutch wealth tax mentioned).

5.9 Long March to Freedom: the Tax Planning Funnel

The tax rates of the common taxes, mentioned above, differ widely. Personal income is taxed at the highest rates (minus various personal allowances). Dividends and royalties are often taxed at lower rates as compared to personal income. Capital gains are taxed at an even lower rate. Of course, this varies by country, but you get the point.

You can imagine this as a funnel. If you're currently a high-taxed salary worker, you could try to arrange your affairs in such a way that a lower tax applies on your income. This can be done by pursuing low taxed business ventures, making use of tax breaks, and of course by international tax planning. Your goal is to get to the bottom. And if you keep reading, you'll discover ways to eliminate this funnel all together (and the paperwork as well).

Tax Planning Funnel

+50%
Now bend over...

35-45%
You're a loyal pet

10-25%
Good boy!

0-10%
EUREKA!
You're free!

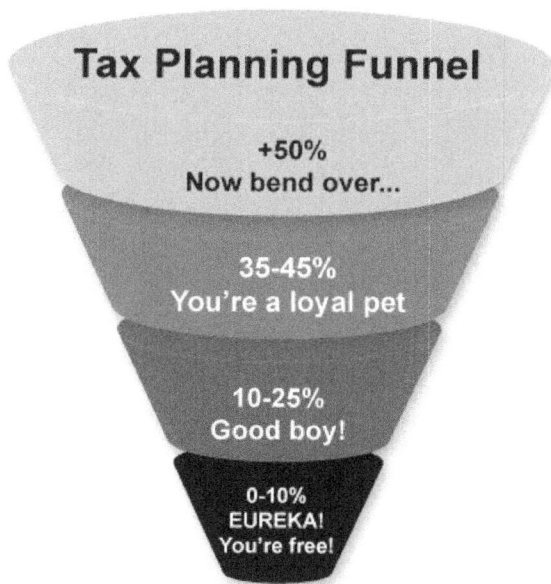

5.10   Offshore Companies, Real or Utopia?

Coincidentally, I encountered three Dutch entrepreneurs who had engaged a particular agent. I heard and read about this agent. The owner was arrested for various forms of tax evasion and fraud. After jail, he changed the name of the company and continued selling offshore companies from the same address. In essence he says that all you have to do to avoid Dutch taxes is to set up a corporation in the UK. It is bullshit, but telling people what they want to hear works: *"stop paying taxes like the royal family."*

Setting up an offshore company alone is normally not enough to lower your tax bill. Most Western countries tax income regardless of its source. It doesn't matter if your income comes from the Berlin, the UK, or the Cayman Islands; it's taxed the same.

Moreover, a whole set of (new) rules aims to prevent these kinds of artificial constructions. These types of regulations can apply to offshore companies: PE, CFC, and General Anti Avoidance Rules.

5.10.1 Permanent Establishment Rules

One essential concept in international taxation is the Permanent Establishment (PE). It helps tax authorities determine where the source of income is, and gives them right to levy. According to the OECD Model Tax Convention,[44] PE means:

"a fixed place of business through which the business of an enterprise is wholly or partly carried on"

The central question is: *where do the actual business activities take place.* The following are accepted aspects of the PE, according to the same Convention:

- *place of management;*
- *a branch;*
- *an office;*
- *a factory;*
- *a workshop, and*
- *a mine, an oil or gas well, a quarry or any other place of extraction of natural resources.*

CIs don't own mines or factories (it refers to actual mining, not Bitcoin mining). However, they are usually the only person managing a company, creating a "place of effective management" wherever they perform these activities. Going back to our example, the Dutch tax authorities can argue that such a UK Company is a Dutch tax payer through its Dutch PE, and tax it accordingly. Oops!

The permanent establishment is a leading tool for tax collectors to prevent tax evasion. It allows them to interpret facts instead of reading what's on the paper. You simply cannot use a basic offshore registration for a business you manage from a high-tax country and stop paying taxes.

Sometimes, business owners use a local director called a nominee. On paper, this person usually manages the company in the country of registration. This is to prevent the above mentioned "place of management." However, if this director is an artificial construct without real power, and the owner still de-facto runs the company by taking all decisions, it *might* not pass scrutiny. Legislations usually apply to direct, and <u>indirect</u> control. The company should be run relatively autonomously by the director (he takes the crucial decisions).

A PE is not a black and white issue. If you temporarily run a business while abroad, you don't establish a PE. The OECD commentary states that a certain degree of permanency is needed for a PE to be established, and generally a PE isn't established in under six months.[45] You shouldn't have PE problems managing a corporation as a CI if you move a lot.

For a State to gain taxing rights, it first must establish that a PE exists. Outside of the Western world, they quite frankly don't care about this for small business owners. Having said this, (some) offshore banks and exchanges now maintain registers of the residence of directors to at least have an indication of where management and control takes place. This information is also exchanged with tax authorities. More on financial transparency later.

5.10.2 CFC Rules

CFC rules empower a State to tax its resident taxpayers on income derived by foreign entities controlled by them.[46] This solely prevents the registration of foreign companies to avoid taxes. CFC rules are not applied in the same way by every country and not all countries even have them. They can be applied in certain circumstances, such as the involvement of tax havens or apply to holding companies with only passive income. This merely applies to CIs owning an offshore company while being a tax resident in a country with CFC rules. Again, this is mostly an issue in high-taxed countries.

5.10.3 General Anti-Avoidance Rules

General Anti-Avoidance Rules (GAAR) affect very few CIs. They are *"domestic rules that allow the tax authorities to re-characterize a transaction or a series of transactions that have been entered with the (sole or main) purpose of obtaining undue tax benefits."*[47]

In times past, one could easily set up a company in Cyprus to hold shares in a mainland European company. Due to the European parent-daughter directive, dividends paid to Cyprus were tax free. Cyprus doesn't tax foreign sourced income nor outgoing dividends. Using Cyprus, one "extracted" dividends tax free from Europe to Cyprus and then to an offshore company. Recently, GAAR has put an end to this. If a company is setup for the sole purpose of realizing such a tax benefit, the source countries can now tax the outgoing income. Moreover, it has become hard to establish a company with a bank account in Cyprus if no real activity takes place there. In short, this gate is being closed.

Congratulations, this was the hard part! Now the fun starts...

6.   <The Road to the Citadel_

Most people never move from the place they were born. They go to school, follow the norms, choose from the available careers, and pursue a "stable" path. They mold their life into conventional and predictable patterns, remaining among old friends and family who remind them of their limitations and their place in life. They accept that these are the cards they were dealt. Perhaps some live in quiet desperation thinking to themselves, *"is this all?"* The uneventful years start moving faster, and everyone around them grows older. One fine day, while mowing the lawn, they feel a sting, and keel over. Their heart fails on the way to the hospital. When their lives flash before them... nothing.

Maybe, you were lucky enough to be the one person born in the best place on earth. But I can tell you that it is a wide world, with lots of options worth exploring. Excessive familiarity with surroundings kills your spirit and breeds laziness in the mind. It denies you a life full of potential. The idea of discovering places, meeting new people, having unique experiences and trying your luck at a business venture excites you. Trying new things keeps you young, alert, and stimulated!

The chance of a fulfilling life and the call for adventure is not the only goal. For those truly seeking freedom and independence, there are other reasons to look across borders. By living in one country you place all your eggs in a one-State-basket: you bet everything on its success. This is a big mistake...

6.1 Spread and Dissolve: International Diversification

Certain things stick with you: a piece of news you hear, a story. I remember vividly sitting on the couch with my mom watching the news. The year was 2001, and the topic Argentina. Since the local currency was a poorly managed piece of shit, anybody with savings had a USD account. During the crisis, the government decided that USD holdings were no longer redeemable. From one moment to the next, savers lost all they had.

The Argentineans were in the street. Old ladies banging pots and screaming. One man stood in front of an ATM as if he lost a child. Others stood silent, defeated. "How can they do this? I lost everything!" said another man while staring oblivious into the camera. I was shocked.

I visited Argentina 10 years ago. They told me: *"we don't trust the government, we don't trust banks."* Every Argentinian with money keeps it out of Argentina. They use banks in Miami and Uruguay, out of reach of their bankrupt and incompetent government. They are conscious about not keeping their eggs in one basket. Especially not in a place with a track record of plundering their citizen's wealth.

I get it now. But these lessons sail by the general population. There always seems to be the notion of "this cannot happen here." Our hometown is the best in the universe; our banks are the safest in the world; our pension fund or social safety net is solid; and our government can fly to the rescue, waving a magic wand, sparkling a universal basic income into existence.

My friends tell me banks in the Netherlands are safe, when a decade ago all the major ones failed and had to be bailed out by the tax payers. A colleague in Cyprus lost two thirds of his pension (400k EUR) thanks to storing it in two Bank of Cyprus accounts. Yellow-vests in France tell a familiar tale when interviewed: pensions cut, taxes increased, hospitals and services disappearing. Pension funds in the US are massively underfunded. Greeks face terrible austerity. And if the next financial crisis happens, EU wide regulation obliges banks to ~~plunder~~ "bail-in" customer accounts first before governments jump to the rescue.[48] This happens not in faraway obscure countries, but RIGHT NOW in the heart of Western civilization.

We are far more like Argentina in 2000 than we want to admit, but I guess we have to learn the hard way. Not you! Now that you picked up this book you can start protecting yourself. How? By diversifying yourself, and your finances internationally. Become a resident in a place where you aren't propping up a failed welfare system. Start a business in a country which is booming. Switzerland, Singapore, Liechtenstein, Panama, and Dubai have banks which survived massive crises without bankruptcies. Store gold in a safe in Austria; it waits for you there no matter what happens to the economy. Grow your own food in the middle of nowhere, where the local population doesn't form mobs and pull down statues if their feelings are hurt. And of course, emerge yourself in the decentralized revolution. Even if nothing goes wrong in your life, adopting the tactics below is like carrying a spare tire when driving in the desert: common sense. Moreover, it can be highly profitable.

The flexibility and mobility inherent in being a CI allows you to optimize your life for freedom and security. You don't have to be swept along in currents of hysteria caused by forces beyond your control. You earn "Individual Sovereignty" by learning how to find those places where the system protects you rather than threatens you. You can refuse to play by rules you find personally offensive, inconvenient, or immoral. Move your ass and your assets out of the arena. Climb to the highest ring of the Colosseum of life, order a cool fresh drink from those sweet smiling eyes, and observe the carnage below: "Wow, interesting."

If you want to take steps to free yourself from society, regulations and taxes you have to start looking across borders. And the way to do this: Flag Theory.

6.2 The Elite's Closest Guarded Secret: Flag Theory

Countries welcoming to entrepreneurial and ambitious individuals exist. By structuring your life around such countries, by "planting flags," you can reap the international diversification benefits mentioned.

The concept was first mentioned in 1964 by Harry D Shultz in his book *"How to Keep Your Money and Your Freedom."* The original concept was comprised of three flags: (1) a second passport, (2) a safe location for your assets outside your own country and (3) a legal address in a tax haven.[49]

Dr. W. G. Hill later coined the term "Flag theory," and refined the idea of the "PT" a permanent traveler—also known as a perpetual tourist. He added an additional two flags: (4) a place of business, and (5) playgrounds (where you enjoy yourself). The end result:

(1) Passport and Citizenship – becoming a free citizen not "controlled" by one State
(2) Business Base – where you earn tax free money
(3) Residence and Domicile – living in a tax haven
(4) Asset Management – where you invest and store your wealth
(5) Playgrounds – where you spend your money

With the invention of the internet, writers on this topic included a sixth flag; (6) the electronic haven: cyber-sovereignty and privacy. Franky, authors over the years have applied the theory of flag theory based on their personal preferences, the needs of their clients, or the fees they make on their products. For example, second citizenships are often touted as an essential tool for freedom. In my opinion, this is mainly for those from developing countries with poor travel documents or those with an aggressive government. For "regular" people, the quickest gains are made by shifting residency. Feel free to create your own list of what *you* think is important.

As of late the crypto community has been meming about a place called The Citadel where they can hide with their wealth, protected by great walls while the world falls into chaos. The Citadel, however, is not a place: it is many places at once!

For the remainder of this book, I reprioritized flags according to the needs of CIs. Furthermore, I added a specific flag for bank accounts since access to financial services is such an essential but complex aspect of the CI lifestyle.

This resulted in the following seven flags:

(1) Legal residence – Where you live tax-free
(2) Business base – Where and how you earn your money
(3) Financial services – How you get paid
(4) Asset haven – Where you keep your assets safe
(5) Passport and citizenship – Second Citizenship
(6) Playgrounds – Where you spend your money
(7) Electronic haven – Cyber-sovereignty and privacy

Don't worry if you have no flags yet. It's not a science or a hard goal. You don't need all flags to improve liberty. Maybe one flag is enough. Two or three flags are better than one! It's something more than a lifestyle. It's a state of mind. A life-long process.

The remainder of this book is devoted to how to plant these flags. We take the perspective of the crypto investor, and let international (tax) law be our guide. Enthusiastic writers attributed a separate flag status to cryptos themselves. After all, they allegedly exist independently of one nation's control. Although this is true, let us not forget the section on legality of cryptos; you as a person own the cryptos, and are thus subjected to taxes and claims. Cryptos are a crucial tool in the journey to sovereignty, but on their own they don't provide the jurisdictional protection flag theory advocates.

6.3   How Little You Need Might Surprise You

Flag theory and permanent travel was designed with the ultra-rich and independently wealthy in mind. But for the modern CI, it is difficult to avoid flag theory! The best bank accounts, online payment systems, business registrations, and freelance jobs are rarely found in ones' hometown. When consciously applying flag theory, however, you don't just use what works. You walk the extra mile and actively structure your life to ensure optimal freedom and prosperity. This means: low taxes, control over your assets, and legal protection of what's yours.

One myth is that you need to be wealthy or earn a large income to benefit from tax planning. This comes from the times when it was possible to setup a "mail-box" company with minimum substance and benefit from tax treaties. One needed a certain amount of income to justify the legal and administration costs. But moving to a better tax system doesn't have to be expensive. Certain countries allow you to (temporarily) live there by extending tourist visas. The crucial element of tax planning—your place of residence—can be changed at the price of a bus or airline ticket!

A common excuse is: "I need X (something unrealistic) amount of money before I can be happy/free/travel the world." This is just fear of taking the first step. In many pleasant countries, the cost of living is far lower than what you're spending on rent in the developed world. I know a Cuban/German woman who recently visited her 120th country. I asked her how she was able to afford it. She told me she worked at Oktoberfest, making a couple of thousand, and travels the rest of the year for about 500 USD a month and the occasional gig. She stays with friends and coach surfs. She is always contacted by friends saying: "I wish I could afford to travel like you!"

Thousands of globetrotters work casually when they feel like it. Dance teachers, entertainers, English teachers, hotel and restaurant staff, dive instructors, cruise ship or yacht crew, and in thousands of other portable trades and occupations. If they can do it, so can you (especially after the next bull-run).

What else? A bank abroad might be cheaper to use than a bank at home (conversion rate and fee wise). A product you created might be sold cheaper by using a foreign service. If you're young, you might be able to get a cheaper insurance with better coverage in the free market than you have now. And for those looking for quality of life, there are places where there is better service, more modern facilities, and more safety that you are experiencing now.

A low cost of living can have downsides. You have temptations: things you couldn't do before. Massages every day, beach parties, and nice dinners. All this "cheap" entertainment adds up. No work gets done. This is especially a problem for those weak in character. Not being able to resist, they move to Asia or Central America to live the dream, spending way more than back home!

They go broke, and return empty handed (but with a smile on their face). Just remember; a serious CI isn't controlled by circumstances.

6.4 Join the International Fast-Lane

I heard a funny story about a Dutch couple moving to Bali. They had been planning this move for years. They would work online and start a local business. The week before departure they had a farewell party for friends, complete with coconuts, Balinese music, and traditional clothing. In Bali, they rented a house. This is where things started to go wrong. After they paid for their one year contract and settled in, they noticed they had no internet. When trying to get their house connected with a simple wire they ran into a brick wall. They never got it to work and didn't know who to talk to. In addition, they experienced the usual business and visa issues. Before long, they fled back to the Netherlands. Bali wasn't the paradise they imagined it to be.

If you're serious about moving abroad, don't go all in right away. Don't invest financially or emotionally in a certain country or a particular outcome. Your hometown might not be perfect, but it's even more unlikely a city on the other side of the world is. Start by living abroad, maybe only for a few months. Stay on tourist visas and rent by the month. Grow confidence. Don't jump head first into a golden opportunity. Observe. Test if you're happy. Go grocery shopping, get to know prices outside tourist areas, join a gym, get hobbies, and make local contacts. Maybe even do this in a few countries. See what you love most. Make decisions based on experience, not on expectations or suggestions.

This also applies to tax planning. Sometimes people ask me where they should immigrate to. This is like tying a horse behind the cart. I have no problem giving suggestions, but it's hard to know what they will like. Oman doesn't have income tax, but unless you enjoy racing a 4x4 through the desert, it's pretty boring. What's the point of having a tax-free life if you hate it?

Another common mistake? Asking your accountant how you can lower your taxes by moving abroad. There are a number of problems with this. First of all, local accountants, tax advisors, and other "licensed professionals" have no experience with anything but domestic issues, and asking them is mostly useless. They might try to help with vague ideas that no longer work, or they relate it to "Panama Papers" and expect something sinister. And this is not without risk. Across the Western world, service agents, accountants, and tax advisors are now legally obliged to report "suspicious" behavior.[50] If they don't, they risk sanctions. Even when you have no intention of breaking the law, you could end up in an investigation, resulting in nasty hidden records on you.

And let's not forget, even when you hate high taxes, far more people on the other side of the spectrum think taxes are the only thing preventing complete anarchy. They cannot fathom somebody leaving their cult. Best not tell others about your ideas or walk into a random lawyer's office. If you must, establish what you can and cannot say beforehand.

Start your planning well in advance. Understand what you're getting yourself into. Build a support network of like-minded people. It might be frustrating that there aren't exact guidelines explaining your situation. Get over it. Doors open and close all the time. There are lots of options to claim your life back.

As promised, I'll start with the most impactful step: getting a new residence. This is discussed next.

7. <Residence – 1st Flag_

It's said that one of the things you learn when traveling is that everybody is wrong about other countries. I would argue everybody is wrong about their own country as well. No one country is the best place on Earth. They all have benefits and drawbacks. If you're currently living in the Western world, you experience a high standard of living, but also heavy taxes and regulations, bankrupt banks, and underfunded pension systems. If you live in the countryside in Asia nobody bothers you, but the roads might wash away during the rainy season.

Regardless, the first step to regaining freedom and sovereignty is by getting the hell out of your home country. The easiest way? Become a resident of a country with fewer rules and where your income isn't taxed or taxed only a little. Rules differ as to when you become a nonresident. It can be easy, or difficult. But you *can* get out dodge. Your residence, or lack thereof, has enormous impact on your tax bill.

Where to move to reduce your taxes? In order to answer this question, we must first understand the various tax systems.

7.1 Different Tax Systems: Candy Shop for Grown-ups

For the outsider, tax law is complex. Each country over time developed its own taxing strategy. And even though the general concepts are the same, no universal road-map exists. Whenever you want to be sure about your situation, looking at the tax code is the only real option (or have someone look at it).

I have experienced CIs who get frustrated with this; they want a simple answer and move on. But look at it from the bright side: because diverse systems exist, you have options. If the rest of the world would tax as Western Europe does, there would be nowhere to run.

Your task is simple: immigrate to a country with a different tax system. You can pick from a variety of systems; I created a list of seven, plus one non-official option. I provide examples of each, but I am not making a country list (it might be outdated the moment you read this). A Wikipedia page called "international taxation"[51] does a sufficient job in providing details on the first three systems. Never base an opinion on Wikipedia alone though; *always* confirm with official sources.

7.1.1 The Worldwide System

The "Worldwide System" subjects its residents to tax on their worldwide income (derived from sources within, and outside of its territory), and non-residents only on the income derived from its territory.[52] This is the tax system of the majority of States.

As an individual you pay taxes no matter where your income comes from. Examples are Germany, Japan, and Brazil. Not much can be done here, besides local deductions or specific tax strategies.

7.1.2 The Territorial System

The "Territorial System" subjects to tax both residents and non-residents only on the income derived from sources located in its territory. All income derived from sources outside of its jurisdiction is disregarded for tax purposes.[53] Such a system is found in almost all countries in Central America, a number of countries in Asia (such as Hong Kong, The Philippines, and Malaysia) and in various other places.

Where and how you make your money defines your tax planning options here. In order to benefit from such a system you need a (passive) income stream clearly sourced in an offshore jurisdiction. Examples are dividends paid by a foreign company, royalty payments, capital gains, pensions, or rental income. It's essential that those income streams aren't taxed at source. If, for example, you own shares in an online marketing company in the UK, and get paid an annual dividend, this can be enjoyed tax free in territorial systems around the world.

If you start a local business, this income is obviously not foreign sourced, and you'll have to pay taxes on the income generated. If you're a software engineer working from your laptop and invoicing for your services, arguably the source of income (your work) is within the territory—*and taxable.* This area is murky and in practice the majority of territorial systems pursue a rather pragmatic policy; e.g. it only targets those directly participating in their economies by working locally or selling to local clients.

7.1.3 Countries with <u>No</u> Income Tax

"No Income Tax" might sound radical, but two dozen jurisdictions offer just that. Governments collect their funds from various sources such as consumption taxes, registration fees, and natural resources. These are usually small island countries (frequently offshore financial centers) or larger oil-rich countries with monarchies. Immigrants can have a hard time becoming residents in some of these States.

The quality of life in these countries varies considerably, and the cultural differences can sometimes make it hard to settle down. The cost of living and visa process may be a barrier, especially for starting CIs. Examples are the UAE (Dubai), Oman, the Bahamas, the Cayman Islands, and Monaco. It is relatively easy to become a resident in Dubai, but the cost of living is high.

Things are different in such a system. There are, for example, no tax returns, no questions about the source of income, and bookkeeping requirements are minimal. You don't have to report your income, and nobody cares how much you own. Economically, you're pretty much free to do what you want, and it's as easy as moving there.

7.1.4 Remittance Based System

We already touched on the "Remittance Based System" briefly. It's comparable to the territorial system, with the divergence that only money received in the country is taxed. This system applies to those who are residents, but not domiciled in the UK and its former colonies, such as Ireland, Malta, and various overseas territories. This is known as the "non-domiciled system." However, Thailand also has a remittance based system for all Thai tax residents regardless of domicile.[54]

How does this work in practice? As an example, a foreign sourced dividend paid to a non-domiciled Maltese resident on a Maltese bank account would be considered remitted, and thus taxable. The same dividend sent to a bank in Switzerland would be tax exempt. In non-dom States, you could still be liable for social security, consumption taxes, and taxes on locally-sourced income.

Just as the territorial system, where and how you make your money matters. You need a (passive) income stream with a clear offshore source. Examples are dividends paid by a foreign company, royalty payments, capital gains, pensions, or rental income. Those income streams shouldn't be taxed at source.

Obviously, in the non-dom system you'd need to be non-domiciled, which sounds complex, but in practice it's easy. Domicile is partially determined by intention, and intention is hard to prove. The UK, for example, tackles this by looking at the number of years you have lived there to determine if you're deemed domicile (15 years out of the last 20).[55]

An exact definition of remitting doesn't exist, for the simple reason that if it would, people would find ways around it (deliver it in on a trained dolphin). It roughly means: received in the country by whatever means. In practice, there are countries where remittances aren't monitored, turning the remittance based systems into a de-facto territorial system.

7.1.5 Citizenship-Based Taxation

Citizenship based taxation is a system only in use in the Unites States and Eritrea. These two nations tax holders of their passports no matter where in the world they live. This makes these passports the most expensive in the world! Basic deductions can lower the tax burden, but there are always reporting obligations. More for US citizens at the end of this book.

7.1.6 Special Programs Attracting High Caliber Hodlers

Various States have special programs geared towards foreign business owners, wealthy investors, and pensionados. Examples are Switzerland and Liechtenstein, where for an agreed upon lump sum payment all taxes are covered, regardless of the amount of income. Michael Schumacher famously used this arrangement.[56] Other special programs aimed at high caliber individuals who can contribute to the economy are found around the world. An example is Portugal, where for wealthy individuals certain foreign sourced income is exempt from taxes.[57] In addition, the Portuguese tax authorities issued "binding information" to a tax payer, setting the precedent for exempting the buying and selling of cryptos from income taxes, unless you are a professional trader.[58]

7.1.7 Low Tax Countries

Geotaxarbitration does not only cover paying no tax; it can mean paying "Low Tax." Southeastern European countries such as Romania, Bulgaria, Hungary and Montenegro have lower tax rates as compared to Western Europe. Budapest has been a hub for young international entrepreneurs for this reason (15% income tax[59] and a low cost of living).

A new country may result not only in a cozier tax rate, but it also might offer access to tax treaties for better tax planning. In addition, you can experience lower contributions to local governments, less paperwork, and an overall higher standard of living at a lower cost.

7.1.8 The "We Don't Care" Model

Don't tell anyone, but there is an informal eight system called the: *"we don't care about your income as long as you spend it here"* system. There is no interest or infrastructure to go after foreigners, especially temporary ones. Remember, CIs aren't entitled to benefits; they bring money into the economy; and they pay consumption taxes. There is little risk, because these countries have no problem dealing with people who misbehave or overstay their visas. They simply kick them out of throw them in jail.

In many countries, tax discipline is in general not very strict, including for the locals. This rings even more true in rural places, or countries with bigger problems such as frequent ecological disasters or political instability. I am not advocating for grey areas; I'm simply telling you as it is. In many areas in this world, people mind their own business and nobody cares. And you're welcome to join them!

7.2   Robust Tactics for Getting a New Residency

Good. By now you understand the tax systems and picked a favorite country. How can you move there? To stay in the country legally, you must achieve the status of resident. Various methods lead to this status. Countries usually welcome contributing foreigners. A contribution is usually economical, but there are other options. Additional conditions might apply, such as a minimum amount of time spent or renting a local apartment.

A common way to get residency is by getting a work permit. Almost all countries offer the status of resident to those with a local job. Having certain locally required qualifications can offer a fast-track to new residents, which is often determined on a point system such as in Australia and Canada.

Studying is another option leading to residency. This can be in a traditional university, but it doesn't have to be. Thailand and Indonesia offer residence permits for those studying the language or culture.

Family ties or relationships can be another foundation for residency, either through marriage, or by being descended from a citizen. Religious and political beliefs can also serve as the basis for residency.

Self-employed CIs can pick up residency by starting a local business. This can be restricted to specific fields or where there is a local need. Sometimes it's required to employ a minimum amount of locals.

Self-supporting retirees are accepted or even actively recruited by countries such as Panama, Philippines, Costa Rica, and Malaysia. In the Philippines, you can pick up a pensioners permit from the age of 35 with their SVVR program.[60]

7.3 Staying on Tourist Visas

You might not desire to invest the time, money, and effort into getting residency. In this case, you can stay somewhere on a tourist visa. Georgia issues a one year tourist visa. In the Philippines you can extend a tourist visa up to a year without having to leave the country. Thailand even offers an "Elite" tourist visa, with validity of up to 20 years (annual exits and quarterly reporting of your whereabouts are obliged).

Popular countries such as Indonesia and Malaysia allow shorter stays, but CIs then do so-called "visa runs." This means you leave the country and come back the next day. A new visa is stamped into your passport, and the time starts over again.

This tactic has limits. I have heard from people whom after a number of visa runs were refused entry in either Thailand, Malaysia, or Indonesia. If you want to stay permanently, you need a residency permit. Don't break the restrictions placed on tourist visas. Don't overstay visas (not even a day). Never work locally.

Obviously, not everybody adheres to this advice. Large numbers of yogis, dance instructors, and martial arts teachers travel across the world performing their craft. There are, however, departments actively searching and deporting them—think hipsters dashing through Balinese rice-fields after a barbershop raid. Dance schools in Jakarta regularly hire foreign teachers for workshops, attracting the attention of immigration officers, sometimes tipped by jealous competitors. Conversely, a famous co-working space in Chiang Mai was visited by police and everybody had to prove they weren't working for a local company. It turned out nobody was, and they left. There's a lesson here somewhere...

It is sometimes said that working or trading on a laptop constitutes a breach of visa restrictions. But this is not a black or white issue. Every business man nowadays has a laptop. Is sending a few emails considered work? Is building a website for a business on the other side of the world? Is writing a book no one reads? From my observations in Asia, the authorities consider serving local clients as working locally. What you do on your laptop is your own concern.

One special comment has to be made for the Corona Virus. What we saw in 2020 was a massive restriction on our "freedoms" to travel. These were snapped away in an instant. For those heavily relying on tourist visas, life stopped. Tourists weren't allowed access anywhere, cutting them from homes and loved ones. Those with official residence permits faced fewer problems (some were kept out as well). Although it is still difficult to see where this will lead, this too will pass. Nevertheless, it remains an argument for ensuring proper residency arrangements.

7.4   Moving within the EU

For CIs from Europe, we have to discuss one of the fundamental principles of the European Union: the principle of Freedom of Movement. Citizens from EU countries are free to move to other EU countries. If they weren't, the EU would not work, and this principle is vital to the EU. In practice, requirements apply, such as a rental contract, proof of employment, or a business registration in order to be registered as a resident.[61]

Officially, you're not allowed to stay longer than three months in a country without becoming a resident according to the requirements mentioned above. In practice, I know of no practical enforcement of this. You can move to another EU country, rent a short term apartment, and enjoy life. To me this is a matter of principle. If Eastern European criminals can roam my parents' neighborhood stealing everything not bolted down, I can surely go to Eastern Europe and write a book in a coffee shop.

But remember: by moving below the radar you don't relieve yourself of tax obligations. Individual member States have rules determining when you become a tax resident. If you meet these qualifications, you have to pay taxes regardless of whether you're registered or not. I had one clever entrepreneur tell me that since there are no border checks in the EU no one can prove that you were in the country. Sure, but then you can't prove you weren't! I would advise to either register or stay for only a short period to not trigger any obligations. And don't take a local job (such as in a bar) because this type of income is taxable right away across Europe.

7.5   The Great Escape: Giving up Tax Residency

If you were born in a country, have lived there your entire life, been a tax payer, and have your economic and social life there, you cannot simply pack up your bags and leave. You need to figure out what is needed to release the tentacles of your country of origin; this is the <u>most important</u> step!

Since every country has unique rules regarding taxation, they have different rules on when you can stop paying. Your current financial and business situation also determines if becoming a nonresident is easy or not. Some authorities are stricter than others.

CIs tend to start traveling first, and figure everything out along the way. They talk to me after they pay too much in taxes or run into difficulties. I also see CIs who can't compare the benefits of investing in a new residency now (difficult/expensive) to the benefits over the coming years. Or they keep things as they are and tell themselves taxes are too boring or too difficult. They would rather work six months a year for benefits they don't enjoy!

Countries can make it easy to leave. An example is Germany, where you have to de-register and make sure you don't have a domicile or a customary place of abode.[62] Others, such as the UK, have a time test and if a former resident spends less than 16 days in the UK for three years, he is no longer considered a tax resident.[63]

In the eyes of some tax authorities, former residents remain tax residents for a number of years, unless they go through an elaborate process and cut all ties. An example is Finland, where a Finnish citizen is still considered to be resident in Finland until three years have passed from the end of the year when the individual left the country, unless he proves no essential connections with Finland have been maintained.[64]

Moving to a known tax haven specifically might not work. A Spanish national who gives up Spanish tax residence is nonetheless considered a Spanish tax resident for the year of departure and the next four tax years if the new tax residence is in a tax haven.[65] And Italian citizens who claim to be nonresidents in Italy have their claims of tax exemption denied if their new country of residence is a tax haven.[66]

If you are a resident of a country with strict exit rules, you always have the option of becoming a tax resident in a country with a tax treaty with your current country of residence. Because remember: tax treaties limit the rights of tax authorities to tax you!

7.5.1 Can You Keep Your House?

Having a house available to you is a key factor in determining taxing rights. This is both true on the domestic level, as with tax treaties.[67] Keeping your house or buying a holiday home could create tax liabilities. If you own your residence, you can rent it out. If you currently rent a room, you should let the lease expire. Definitions generally are broad and aimed at establishing facts. A room rented for cash or even a keeping a room in the family home can also be considered a residence.

An essential concept is permanency. A temporary arrangement, such as short term rentals or holiday homes, is not permanent. Of course, "temporarily" living somewhere for years on end is not possible.

7.5.2 Center of Economic or Vital Interests

In tax law, you encounter the term "center of economic or vital interest." This concept can be found occasionally in domestic tax laws, and it is a standard inclusion in tax treaties to determine which of two States has its taxing rights limited.

Economic interests are factors such as the location of a job, business, investments, bank accounts, and insurance. Vital interests can be where your family, spouse or children live, where you have registrations for your car and other possessions, memberships of clubs, and political parties.

7.5.3 Tax Residency Scale

CIs are often binary thinkers. Ones and zeros. They think tax residency is binary as well; you either are, or you're not. As long as they're staying "less than 180 days" in a country all is fine. This is wrong. It helps to see tax residency as an old-school balancing scale.

During the course of your life, you place weights on this scale. These can be heavy weights, such as owning a house, starting a family, or having a job or business. Examples of lighter weights are: where you bank, where you are a member of clubs or organizations, where you are insured, where your car is registered, or where you hold investments. One heavy weight can tip the scale on its own. The lighter weights cannot do this, but might help tip the scale one way or the other in case of uncertainty.

Tipping this scale depends on domestic law, tax treaties and how heavy the weights are. There can be unpredictable influences such as the current political wind or the opinion of a tax inspector. However, you can remove weights that tip the scale to your detriment. Or, you can ensure your scale is so heavily weighted to one side (of your choosing), it cannot be tipped over.

It isn't always easy to determine tax residency. Facts matter, opinions don't. Every situation is unique, and no single approach exists.

7.5.4 Bye Bye! What to do When Leaving

Giving up tax residency from your home country is the only step with real eminent risk. Court cases result from tax payers not clearly moving. This can mean not creating sufficient ties in a new country, or (secretly) keeping ties with the home country. Their exit is murky. Remember: what you say or think is irrelevant. You need proof.

As mentioned, in some countries you get on a plane and leave. Bye-bye! Others demand evidence you moved to a new country of residence. If you currently reside in a country with such strict exit procedures, you need two things: an overview of steps taken and proof of these steps.

In practice, this is simple. You create a folder on your desktop called "Emigration." In it, you create a text file with all steps and dates, for example: "Notified tax authorities about emigration, September 17" or "obtained new residency permit, January 5." Next, you can save scans of documents supporting your case, such as letters, rental contracts, utility bills, local residence permits, tax returns, registrations at local gyms and clubs, local ID or driving license, and passports stamps. This isn't much work, and results in a few MB of files. Make a backup, as tax authorities look back longer than you can remember dates and locations.

Whenever communicating with (tax) authorities, do it in writing and in a traceable way. Use email over phone, and save copies of emails. When sending a letter, use registered mail or a courier. Save a scan of the receipt in your folder. Your position is stronger if backed by facts. Despite what they want you to believe, tax authorities don't have all the information. In fact, they're highly disorganized and make wild assumptions. If you have your house in order, their assumptions can be swept aside easily.

These steps might seem excessive. And most CIs don't document anything, even when they have an unclear story. It is not uncommon for them to move back home after a few years. It helps when you can prove what happened in between, and not leave anything to chance.

Make sure you don't receive benefits you're no longer entitled to, such as welfare or support programs for rent or health care. You might need to pay this back (with fines) and it keeps you in the system.

Having said this, a proper emigration leaves little incentive for chasing you. Migrants move between countries by the millions each year. Audits rarely happen. What I wrote here might be overkill, but see it as insurance.

7.5.5 Emigrating With a Business or (Digital) Assets

Giving up residency can be unbelievably easy when young and without attachments. This changes when you own a business, or assets such as real estate. There are countries with exit or emigration taxes. An example is Canada, where it's called a "deemed disposition."[68]

Even immaterial assets such as intellectual property can induce a tax liability. A Dutch entrepreneur gained exposure by making twelve websites in twelve months while traveling the world. Luckily for him, his websites became popular, and allowed him income to keep traveling. His problem was that he always remained registered as a sole proprietorship in the Netherlands. Income through such a registration is taxed at the highest brackets. Upon emigration, a "fictive sale" occurs and the business is taxed as if sold at current value. He complained loudly about this online, but of the hundreds of ways to structure his affairs, he choose the worst. Try to create and keep intellectual property offshore.

I always advise CIs to emigrate as soon as possible. But as I told you, most CIs only contact me *after* their alt-coin speculation has gone up 500x and they now face a large tax-bill.

If your assets are substantial, you need to be informed about possible exit taxes BEFORE moving yourself, or your business, offshore. Try to understand what is required. Whenever you maintain a business back home and only move yourself offshore, this company might still be obliged to pay taxes on its income and perhaps even on income paid to you. Economic ties can as well be a factor in determining if you (as an individual) remain a tax resident or not.

Tax planning might take more effort in such a case, but the rewards outweigh the hurdles. Even if with your current income streams no tax benefits can be made, perhaps future endeavors can be structured efficiently. Think long term.

7.5.6 Do You *Really* Have to Live There?

Let's get one thing clear: if you become a resident, it doesn't mean you're forced to live there. You only have to become *resident for tax purposes*. You can still travel around. Maybe you stay part of the year? The further you move out into the wide world, the more you can bend (not break) the rules in your favor.

Let's not forget flag theory! Consider if you want to live there, if you want to use it as a business hub, or if you want to use it solely for tax purposes. If the situation demands it, you can become a resident in a low tax jurisdiction first when exiting a high tax jurisdiction. Of course, when you move on nobody bothers you since you were not a regular tax-payer anyway.

You can be considered a resident for tax purposes without having an official residency. This prevents living in a country "under the radar" and not paying taxes when you're supposed to. Logically, this can be turned around; one cannot live on tourist visas and obtain all the evidence needed to prove immigration or residency to a tax authority.

7.6 Always on Vacation

A residence permit is neither necessary nor always desirable. No universal law obliges you to be a formal resident anywhere. You could be a tourist forever. Residence permits require invasive procedures, such as finger-printing and health and background checks. It demands effort, and it forces you to deal with bureaucracy. It might create other restrictions, obligations, or limitations to your freedom. Moreover, it can cost thousands to maintain. And what is the real benefit?

In virtually all countries across the world you can rent an (short term) apartment. You deal with the landlord only. Sometimes they are expected to report foreigners. As long as you hold yourself to the dates on your visa, and you don't break the conditions under which this visa is issued, you're good to go. Foreigners with independent means are rarely bothered.

A common question is what country of residence to fill in on immigration forms. First, nobody ever reads or cares what you fill in. If this makes you uneasy, know that in a large part of the world families live together. Filling in the address of your parents is perfectly okay. I had a client who told me he panicked when the customs agent asked where he lived. He told them he lived nowhere, and they shrugged. Custom agents ask random questions to look for signs of nervousness or inconsistencies. They are firstly interested in smugglers and illegals, and not your tax residency.

One day I received an email from a guy who had not been a resident anywhere for five years and didn't pay taxes anywhere. He wonder if he would "go to jail" in Canada, since he was planning on moving there. This is a perfect example of making things bigger than they are. The Canadian tax authorities cannot jail him since he wasn't subjected to Canada's laws! Moreover, tax matters are firstly considered a civil affair (with possible fines). It only becomes a criminal case (with possible jail time) when it can be "proven beyond a reasonable doubt" that he "intentionally contravened Canadian tax laws in order to evade taxes."[69] This is not the case. Of course, he has to declare all future income in his tax returns and pay what is required.

Some CIs want everything "official" and by the book. They doubt simple low profile techniques offer enough protection. With this mindset, having an official (long term) legal residence is a must. Financial service providers and other parties are now by law obliged to inquire into your residency status. Their questions aren't a threat from a legal perspective, even though they are sometimes perceived as such (banks cannot force you to be a resident somewhere). Since it determines access to the financial system, this is definitely a serious practical hurdle.

Luckily: *"Bitcoin fixes this!"*

8. <Business Base – 2nd Flag_

If you want to become a real CI and enjoy the world, you need money. I have encountered CIs who made a killing by buying early and hodling, and were supported by their wealth. Regardless, the vast majority of CIs make money to support their lifestyle—either by working over distance, trading, or running their own business.

The way you make money has a large effect on tax planning. Your ideal business base (Flag 2) depends on your residence (Flag 1). Flag 1 tells you what kind of income can be enjoyed tax free. Next, you can plant Flag 2 to enjoy such benefits. There are CIs with established businesses or with business models that force one to be in a certain time zone. In these cases, Flag 2 might restrict Flag 1 options. In Dubai, registering Flag 2 is the normal road to Flag 1.

The matching of Flag 1 and 2 options has become a focus point for generalist consultants such as myself. Local accountants and tax advisors normally struggle advising on this—especially when the word "blockchain" is mentioned. They focus on specific domestic or international issues, at which they are better equipped than generalists. In addition, they tend to give advice based on theory, and not what is practically possible.

Frustration can be experienced by CIs whose situation requires a mix of generalist and specialist knowledge to solve. An example of this is a CI emigrating while still involved in complex business activities back home.

Nobody understands everything. This is a reason why I say that you need to get a handle on the basics yourself in order to oversee a variety of opinions.

In this chapter, you'll learn more about the options you have for structuring your business activities and the pitfalls you'll encounter. It's a basic explanation on (offshore) corporations and how to operate them legally. This is a guide as to where to setup a business.

8.1 What's Your Brilliance?

How you make money highly influences what you can and cannot do in terms of tax planning. A first question I always ask is: how do you generate income?

Some CIs I've encountered sell services. They work for a fee per hour as a developer for an exchange, or are paid by assignment—selling their time for money. They sign a contract or send an invoice and get paid in Bitcoins. This model is straightforward and flexible. It allows for simple tax planning, for example by changing residency. You can setup a simple legal entity for this kind of activity, but this is not mandatory.

Others are part of more serious businesses with multiple shareholders. In such a case, there are practical considerations if you want to register a company. You'll need to take into account such things as the need to access the financial system, the level of privacy, or the image of the jurisdiction. Panama is a safe haven that is politically stable with a solid banking system. However, not everybody is excited about wiring funds there. One might expect a field such as international tax to be an area of logic and reason, but tribalism and gut feelings reign supreme.

There are those selling goods and services online. If besides accepting cryptos, the acceptance of credit cards and the use of payment processors is needed, this severely limits where a business can be setup. More on this later.

8.2 Bold New Income Streams

When I started as an international entrepreneur, I had one continuous remote-working assignment and an undeveloped consultancy business. It was a plunge in the deep. I focused all my attention on my main assignment. Nine months in, I received an email telling me I was invoicing too much, and I received a maximum allowance of about 40% of my last invoice, which was not even a livable wage in Asia. I had to scramble for new sources of income, all the while frustrated with myself for letting it get to that point.

I forgot my true goal of economic independence: securing reliable ways to put food on the table. And I realized that just as you diversify investments, you can diversify everything else. Although this reaction came logically to me, most think otherwise. They put all their eggs in one basket: a job. Yes, by specialized and focused work you can make a great living. But when you lose your job, you're screwed. It's a circus act without a safety net. It goes right every day until one day you slip and plunge to your financial death, crushing a happy clown and an alcoholic ballerina.

Entrepreneurship is considered a risk, but done right you become mobile, flexible, and resilient—even when ~~most~~ some of your ideas don't work. One client. One source of income. One business. One product. One method of receiving payments. One debit-card. One passport. One residency. One bank account. One coin. One wallet. Each of those may result in disaster if something happens.

If you still depend on one source of income, don't be discouraged. It's a process. Somewhere along the way you become diversified. Even better, when applying the principles of this book, you'll profit from income streams in multiple countries, in multiple markets, and via multiple systems, and in multiple (crypto) currencies.

Prevent "golden shackles:" a job you secretly despise after coming to depend on the large paycheck. Be able to pack your suitcase and either take your income with you (in a laptop), or happily leave it behind. Real freedom is when you can walk away from anything you no longer enjoy. Protect what no money can buy: time.

8.3 The Genesis Block of Business: the Corporation

When starting a business, the first question is if you should incorporate. A corporation is effectively recognized under the law as a person separate from you. A corporation has the right to own property, hire staff, take on loans, and engage in contracts. It can sue and be sued. A corporation allows investors to invest capital without risking bankruptcy and without the need to be part of day-to-day management.[70]

Running a business means incurring risks: it can go bankrupt, be sued, or end up in a dispute between shareholders. A corporation offers "limited liability" to its shareholders, since they're only liable for the amount they put up in share capital, allowing them to either invest in or run a business while keeping their personal assets safe.

Standard limited liability companies issue shares. Those shares are easily transferable, either as a whole or in smaller amounts. This makes it easy to raise funds by selling a minority part of the shares.

As mentioned, a corporation is a separate person for the law. It has its own income (profit), and is taxed on its own. A corporation pays out profits that are called dividends. Dividends are typically taxed at a lower rate than personal income such as salaries. Certain costs can be deducted: if you need a laptop perhaps the company can purchase it (before tax). Interestingly enough, not all corporations are taxed at source on income or dividends, which allows for tax planning. More on this below.

A corporation can be used as an extra layer of protection against aggressive creditors, ambitious lawsuits, governments, thieves and scammers. You can set up a corporation to keep your personal name out of public registers. This is also handy for not having to use your own name, address, and telephone number on websites. Having Ltd. or Inc. after your company's name also adds a touch of credibility.

A downside of a corporation is that there are costs to start and maintain it, even when you're having a bad year. And while simple limited liability companies in the West are cheap to maintain, trade licenses in Dubai cost thousands of EUR. Moreover, a corporation comes with responsibilities and reporting requirements. You might need to file annual accounts. If you don't know how, you need to hire help.

Sometimes a corporation doesn't make sense. I met an investor who wanted to set up a structure to hold real estate. The annual profit of the rental income would be largely spent on annual fees. I've encountered entrepreneurs spending more on annual fees than they gained in tax savings.

8.4   How to Run a Corporation like a Pro

As mentioned, a corporation acts as a person in the business world with its own interests. In general, it has people involved in three distinct roles: a shareholder invests capital and is entitled to the profits. Next, a director is responsible for the day-to-day management of the company. And finally, a company secretary is responsible for maintaining a record of all decisions and outstanding liabilities of the corporation.

In large companies, this division of roles is familiar: a board of directors takes all the decisions, and every quarter the investors are informed in a shareholders meeting. The board of directors has the power to appoint and remove the person responsible for day-to-day activities, usually the CEO. But the ultimate power lies with shareholders: they appoint the board of directors. A company secretary records and files all the material decisions and changes to the structure.

These concepts are simple, but many small business owners don't get it. They run their business as a sole proprietorship, for example by using company funds to pay for a private "emergency," or by taking decisions on the go without documenting anything. As a single business owner, even though you're one and the same person making decisions, legally speaking you act in distinct roles—*you* the director, signs an employment contract with *you* the individual, to earn a profit for *you* the shareholder.

A company is a separate legal person and only exists on paper. If it makes a decision, it needs to formalize this. This is done by holding a "board meeting" where the directors come together for important decisions, formalized in a "Minutes of Meeting." A director can also pass a "written resolution."

A resolution can be needed to meet legal requirements, for example, when the corporation wants to open a bank account or buy shares of another corporation. Resolutions provide formal records of the company's decisions. They're essential to keeping track of a corporation's commitments and liabilities or to prove ownership of (intellectual) property.

Shareholders hold significant power. The director always has to answer to them, since they can remove him. Be thus careful with offering anyone shares in your business. I often see starting businesses look for capital injections in exchange for shares. One such company was a services agent in Singapore, who was going to register companies using the blockchain (not possible, by the way). The founder raised cash by selling shares and became a minority shareholder. He kept running the operations, but it turned out he was incompetent; the new shareholders removed him. He saw it as being kicked out of "his own" company, and whined about it on Twitter. Remember: ownership is everything.

8.5   Corporation Stacking

A company structure describes the legal way in which a business is structured. A structure can be simple: a corporation with one individual as a shareholder and director. However, big multinationals have a large number of corporations operating under a top holding, informally referred to as a "Christmas Tree." An example of a simple company structure is below.

Example Company Structure

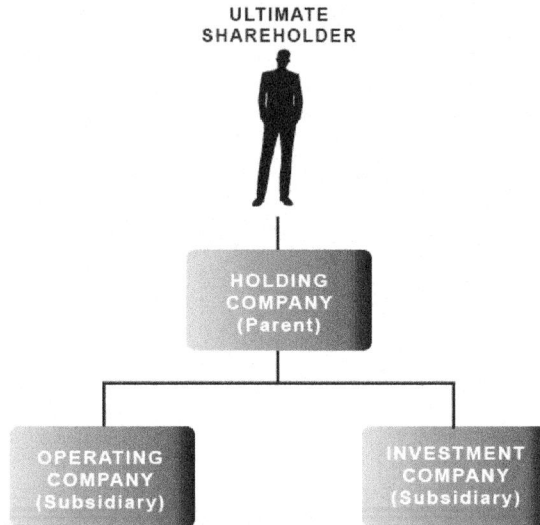

ULTIMATE
SHAREHOLDER

HOLDING
COMPANY
(Parent)

OPERATING
COMPANY
(Subsidiary)

INVESTMENT
COMPANY
(Subsidiary)

Why use holding companies? Operating companies risk claims and lawsuits as a result of actively engaging in contracts and economic activity. Assets kept in a holding company remain out of reach for creditors of the trading company. A holding company combines all your assets under one "umbrella," especially when they're in various jurisdictions. This makes it possible to transfer all business assets with one transfer of shares—instead of having to process the transfer of every asset separately. Sometimes wealthy folks forget this and their heirs need to go through complex legal proceedings in multiple countries.

Holding companies normally don't perform business activities themselves. The reason is simple: if a holding company is sued for its business activities, all the underlying assets are at risk. I was an intern at a real estate firm once and the owner was an appraiser. It turned out later that he practiced appraisal fraud to help secure loans. It blew up in his face, and the firm suffered a massive claim. As the owner, he invoiced from the top holding. The entire business got lost in the proceedings, including the subsidiary real estate company and an insurance business brought in by his business partner.

Holding companies can consolidate and reinvest profits of subsidiaries in a tax efficient manner. Profits distributed to a parent company are often exempt from taxation.[71] If profits stay within a corporate structure, wealth can grow tax free. Ideally, a holding company is a resident in a tax friendly jurisdiction without income tax on foreign sourced income and no withholding taxes on dividends. Examples are Hong Kong, Panama, and Cyprus. Unfortunately, the legislative avalanche has greatly reduced the tax planning use of simple holding structures. Real substance is needed for tax benefits to be had. There are still the non-fiscal reasons of course.

My experience with small international entrepreneurs is that they only use simple structures. Few use holding companies, nor should they. In my opinion, the ultimate goal of tax planning is to get assets free from taxes "in your own name." Using holding companies and complex investment structures add paperwork and costs. Only use them if you have a good reason.

8.6 Payday: How to Cash Out?

When I was working in Dubai, I encountered entrepreneurs who used their corporate bank account for everything: suppliers, office rent, salaries for staff, groceries, tuition for the children, and holidays with their wife. They did not keep books and simply waited for the end of the month to see how much was left. Despite this all, they were relatively successful. They ran into problems when they wanted to sell part of the company (no price can be determined without income statements). They had constant cash-flow problems. It was chaos, actually.

What I learned from this is that whenever no taxes are involved suddenly it matters far less what you do in your economic life. There is no incentive for anybody to care. You're not keeping books? Your problem. Ask yourself: do small entrepreneurs truly need "IFRS compliant" audited accounts to know if their business is successful? I don't think so. It's required because the tax man wants his cut. When you pay less taxes, the administrative burden lessens as a bonus.

Funds generated in a company are owned by a separate legal person. It cannot be used as a cash register by the owners. Whenever funds are transferred from Lowtax Limited to you, the individual, a legitimate reason is needed. The company can pay a profit, pay a salary for services provided, issue a loan, or reimburse expenses made. As discussed earlier, how a corporation pays you affects all tax liability (income tax, dividend tax, etc.).

While ordinary corporations make and receive payments through banks, those active in the decentralized tech can use their own wallets. This has a number of consequences. First of all, there is no need for third-party involvement when making and receiving payments. Secondly, the corporation itself is responsible for both verifying payments and tracking exactly what is owned in which wallet address. And finally, there is the immutable character of cryptos. Those who own the keys, own all the coin. The keys need to be guarded carefully in order to prevent the coins from being stolen. At the same time, this often places all the control over the fund in one person's hand. I have heard of companies in distress where the former staff refused to hand over the keys. The company failed to pay its bills and went bankrupt.

Ideally, you ensure the correct paperwork is in place to prove the ownership of the specific wallet addresses related to the payment. Next, make sure you can substantiate all incoming and outgoing transactions. In case of a dividend, there should be a resolution declaring this dividend. If a salary is paid, there should be an employment agreement or invoices in support of that. If there are incoming payments, there need to be invoices.

8.7   Selecting the Ideal Corporation

As mentioned, I am not going to make a detailed list of places where you can setup your company. Offshore options are shut down all the time, while others emerge. This is especially true with cryptos, where the rules are still in development.

Here is a list of things you can look at when starting a corporation:

- The tax burden from corporate tax (on the company's income and profits) and social security contributions when you pay a salary.

- Are dividends taxed? Often, countries withhold taxes at source on dividend paid to foreign owners.

- Is there VAT? Hong Kong does not have VAT. Yet income tax-free Dubai in 2018 introduced VAT. Foreign VAT is a real cost which cannot be deducted by your foreign clients. No VAT is also easier in terms of bookkeeping.

- How friendly is the jurisdiction towards cryptos? Are there specific requirements?

- Is it simple to open the company? Is it mandatory to have a presence in the country? How much does it cost to set up a company, and what are the necessary procedures? Can it be done in person, or do you need a registered agent? Do you appear on a public record as owner or director?

- How easy is it to administrate your company? Can it be done online? What about audits and bookkeeping? Do you need a license? What is the level of scrutiny for new businesses? Do you need a tax number?

- The safety and reputation of the country. This is especially an issue when you have a B2B business, or you depend on subcontractors in the West. Transactions from certain jurisdictions are more scrutinized than others. Conservative businesses might not want to deal with known tax havens.

- The possibility of opening bank accounts and use of other financial services such as credit card processors. The next chapter discusses financial services.

- Some clients might not be able to wire funds to a bank in an exotic country. They might have to use correspondent banks, which adds to the learning curve. If you have recurring business with one client this is not a problem. But if every payment requires you to send ten emails solving issues, it gets annoying fast (trust me).

There are many variables and every situation is unique. Take your time. Get informed.

8.8 Tax Free Offshore Companies

An offshore company is a company that simply... wait for it... is in another jurisdiction. It does not necessarily mean having a mysterious structure somewhere hidden on a tropical island. If a Canadian person owns a company in the US, he owns an offshore company. If you think about how many foreign companies (indirectly) provide almost everything you own, eat, and use, you understand how much the world relies on offshore services.

Having said that, in this chapter we look at the infamous offshore corporations in places such as the Seychelles, Belize, Nevis, or the British Virgin Islands (BVI). They offer a similar product with slight variations.

First of all, these jurisdictions don't tax income, and have no audits or strict bookkeeping requirements. Starting a business there is relatively easy in terms of paperwork. It's easy to do amendments, such as transferring shares or replacing a director. The costs (when bought directly from registered agents) are low. They are based on standard legal frameworks originated from the BVI and tested in courts around the world.

As a downside we already saw the negative effects of the stigma of traditional tax-free offshore companies. Although it's lawful to operate an offshore company, you'll face practical hurdles. Online payment providers tend to reject legal entities outside of the Western world. Accepting online payments with an offshore company is almost impossible. Your banking options are restricted to other remote jurisdictions, which causes problems with transactions. In the offshore world, a solution that provides a solid reputation, total tax-exemption and is cheap does not exist. You will only ever be able to select two out of these three elements.

And as discussed in previous chapters, modern tax planning relies on substantial activity. Anyone who visited the Caribbean knows little happens there, let alone the activities of 100.000s of offshore companies (all with an address in the same street). This is changing though. For example, the BVI implemented substance conditions (hiring local representation) for certain business activities.

As we saw, the offshore services industry is quickly changing and becoming transparent and subject to regulations. The use of offshore companies with no tax residency, no substance, no filing obligations, and complete privacy has been the focus of this. As a result, banks have stopped opening accounts for traditional offshore companies. But crypto transactions are peer-to-peer. There is no third-party to enforce legislation. This could mean a revival for the use of traditional offshore companies for crypto businesses, since the actual tax rates (0%) did not change.

8.9   Sole Proprietor... or Not?

Starting entrepreneurs oftentimes are under the impression they need to "register a business" to make it "official." This is even before any money has changed hands. Look, there's always a little wiggle room before a business needs to register, as long as you're transparent about the income you make towards the tax authorities. Nobody cares if you sell a few products online and make a bit of income. After you start trading on a more sophisticated level, a business registration is likely needed. Again, it's not a black or white issue, but more like a scale. Registering a business isn't your first concern, but making money is! Figure out if someone is willing to pay for your work or product first.

Also, ask yourself what you do when registering yourself as a sole proprietor. A corporation is a separate legal person for the law; a sole proprietor is not. You're still individually liable for debts or damages. Why bother? Well, the main reason you need to register yourself is again taxation. Business registrations come with bookkeeping requirements and VAT numbers. They allow for governments to see what's going on and tax accordingly.

It's almost a subconscious need for Westerners to register everything and make "100% sure" not to "skirt the law." As if we cannot act without permission of big daddy government anymore. I admit, it took me years to get rid of this mindset. As an international CI you <u>don't need</u> to register a business. A corporation (legal person) can own assets and send invoices, and so can you. Personal bank accounts are easier to open and face less monitoring than corporate ones. You don't have to pay annual agent or accounting fees. And you can focus on doing work and enjoying the pay—*especially at the start of your business.*

Practical requirements remain, such as clients demanding VAT numbers when you need to import goods or when you work with a conservative company having specific demands. And from a tax perspective there is little discussion as to who is liable for taxes (you are).

A crucial argument against doing business in your own name remains: unlimited liability. Unlimited liability means you're open to personal bankruptcy if you're sued because of business activities. If you're at risk for lawsuits or large claims, setting up a corporation remains essential. Only you can determine if your activities carry risk and if you need protection from it.

9.   <Financial Services – 3rd Flag_

Every now and then you see the downplaying of the need for cryptos because existing payment systems work so well. Usually, these people use banks in their daily life, which is centered on one city. Unfortunately, they don't know how dysfunctional the international financial system truly is.

So far I have had accounts frozen asking for documents I could not provide, stranded without cash on the Costa Rican carnival after my card was blocked for "my protection," waited for two years to receive a replacement debit card from a foreign bank, got an account closed I owned for 25 years because my identity wasn't confirmed (I had sent them a copy attested by the Dutch consulate by courier, but they had lost it). I saw payment processor accounts closed because my business was considered a "risk." I had payments rejected when made to a "suspicious" company, and a couple of small payments simply "disappeared" between banks with no means of getting my money back.

And let's talk about transaction and conversion fees. Take for example one of my e-commerce business selling eBooks in USD. First of all, my clients pay 1-2% in conversion if their card isn't in USD. Next, the payment processor takes about 3-5%. For regulatory reasons, my USD income can only be transferred to my corporate bank account in Hong Kong Dollars (I discovered this after I installed everything). My costs for hosting and advertising are charged in USD, and I don't have a HKD personal account. So all income has to be converted back to USD. If I pay myself an income, there is a 12 USD transaction fee. Next, I have to get the money out of the ATM, which again means conversion and transaction fees.

I am constantly optimizing my money flow as to reduce friction, and there are great companies, such as Transferwise, that are helping with that. Luckily, for me, I can access such services. As mentioned, due to regulatory concerns, a payment system like above is often not even available for people in developing countries. They face even larger hurdles and fees.

The problem is, for now, we are stuck with this system. "Bitcoin solves this" is a common expression. But for now, we still highly depend on the international payment system. Moreover, you need the financial system the moment you take your earnings of the table. So let us analyze what we are dealing with.

9.1 Offshore Banking Decoded

For centuries, people stored their money safely and in secret. Pirates buried treasure on deserted islands. European crusaders entrusted their estate to reliable family members. The reasons? Protect it from thieves, malicious creditors, out of control governments, ex-wives, or the eldest son with a weakness for hookers and blow. A great reason for offshore money storage is to keep money safe during political turmoil such as wars, political oppression, and economic crisis. In Venezuela, Argentina, and Zimbabwe the governments (recently) destroyed their local economy and currencies. And many Western countries are now trying their best to copy them.

As discussed, an offshore account is simply a bank account in a different jurisdiction. For all those who travel, work and study in multiple countries, and for businesses operating internationally, having bank accounts in various jurisdictions is normal. If you move abroad, you'll end up with new banking arrangements. You need to receive payments from clients and pay bills in the local currency without insane international transfer fees.

Smart countries realized that when they're friendly to capital, it flows to them. Small countries with little natural resources, such as Switzerland, Hong Kong, Singapore, and nowadays Dubai, benefit from this approach. And certain small exotic islands use offshore financial services as a source of income as well.

Offshore banks have become associated with laundering money and hiding money from the tax authorities. If we believe the general opinion, we would think that traditional offshore banks are filled with piles of black-money delivered on power boats driven by Russian models. Look, fishy things do happen. Regulatory changes over the last ten years, however, had significant impact. Offshore banks are not directly connected to payment systems such as swift. Therefore, they have to work with correspondent and intermediary banks in Europe, where they also hold deposits (itself a risk). These correspondent banks have zero tolerance towards anomalies. Offshore banks are now, in my experience, strict enforcers of AML legislation. They are on top of where the money is going and why.

Traditional offshore banks can be surprisingly stable. Meaning they are 100% capitalized and don't speculate with money. They only hold deposits at a small return at known systemic banks in Europe. As a result, they don't offer interest on accounts, and they charge higher account maintenance and transaction fees. The ones used by SMEs are small and a fraction of the size of known international banks. Albeit in known financial centers such as Switzerland, the Cayman Islands, and Bermuda (branches of) larger banks are found.

9.1.1 FinTech Alternatives

To solve the flaws in the financial system, a new phenomenon emerged: FinTech (Financial Technologies). Companies using technology to address specific shortcomings. An example is Transferwise, which solves international transfers by wiring from and to local banks and settling the transaction internally. Certain FinTech companies now also offer virtual bank accounts.

It is worth noting that they are considered financial intermediaries and subjected to similar regulations as banks. Moreover, they themselves have to use banks to provide their services. This sometimes creates problems, when they themselves lose access to their account due to compliance issues. They are more fickle than banks. Having said that, these are great solutions and are somewhat more flexible in their account opening process. For some, they are the only option left. Alas, they too will be replaced by cryptos.

9.2 Banking Secrecy

When I started in the business services industry, I sat down with one of the partners of the firm. She explained the basics of tax planning and scattered common myths. The first: there is no banking secrecy, even in Switzerland. By then, all jurisdictions had legislation allowing for the exchange of information with tax authorities.

In those days, the government needed a court order to find out who was behind a specific account. Since those day, the international financial sector moved rapidly to complete transparency. What is introduced by the joint efforts through the OECD is the Common Reporting Standards (CRS).[72] The CRS obliges banks to automatically exchange account details with your country of residence. This legislation is introduced in every country you might consider banking, unless you consider storing your savings in a bank in sub-Saharan Africa.

One essential element of the CRS is for financial institutions to exchange the information for the right individual. This is the Ultimate Beneficial Owner (or UBO), or sometimes called Beneficial Owner (BO). This is the person entitled to the benefits of said account. The discovery of the UBO prevents the use of paper structures to hide the identity of the owner by using nominees (shareholders on paper) or trusts and foundations. This is why banks nowadays asks for the one behind the scenes (if any).

One thing needs to be clear: there is NO secret banking. Not anymore. Regardless of what you hear in the media. And these same standards apply to crypto-exchanges.

9.3 Financial Surveillance Shenanigans

Reporting your information to governments is not the only thing financial institutions do. They now monitor for "money laundering" and "terrorist financing." The first thing financial institutions do is run your data through a database of criminal records. The most widely used is World-Check, owned by Reuters. Reuters, of course, is a large news network. I met the head of this organization who proudly told me they had a variety of sources for information. In response to my question on whether this meant that they added anything other than criminal convictions by a judge, such as mere accusations and (fake) news, he told me they were careful to include truthful information. Sure.

Financial service providers are risk averse. If anything is out of the ordinary, they'd rather reject a client than risk another scandal. I helped two French clients, who barely spoke English, register a business. A banker came into the office and they filled in all the forms. The account was never opened. We were never explained why, other than it had to do with World-Check. The clients were never convicted, and they had no idea why they were rejected.

This is the problem with databases: who knows what's in them? Over time they are filled with all kinds of data containing typos, people with similar names, and fake news. One day, I saw a colleague doing a check and filling in all the data of the client, such as passport number, telephone number, and current address. I asked him why he uploaded such sensitive data. There was no why; he just filled in all the blanks. We established that to check for a criminal record (obligation of the registrar) only the bare minimum, such as the name and date of birth, is needed.

Besides the strict gate-keeping, your activity is continuously monitored for "suspicious transactions." What's suspicious is in the eye of the beholder. Author Richard Miller researched court-approved reasons to search individuals and seize their property. Among the reasons were being among the first passengers off an airplane, being among the last passengers off an airplane, and being among the middle group of passengers off an airplane.[73]

If you go through lists of what are considered suspicious transactions by banks, unfortunately much of it applies to CIs.[74] The fact alone you're active in cryptos designates you a risk, even when you're a tax payer and comply with all laws. Risk assessment and monitoring is increasingly done by algorithms. And your access to the financial system is determined by them.

Banks use a freeze first, ask questions later policy. A court order is not needed, a suspicion can be enough. Whenever deemed suspicious, a transaction is on lockdown in no-man's land, and you're asked to supply supporting documentation. If the requested is not provided, a transaction is send back (minus "service" fees, of course). If this happens too often, the account is closed. A bank might be obliged to secretly submit a "suspicion report" with the regulators, adding again all sorts of data related risks. And again, who knows what they report? They might report something for the sake of reporting, since if they don't, they themselves might become suspicious. Private citizens are now monitoring each other, as in former communist East Germany.

This is not only done once. This is done at every financial institution involved in the chain. Let's say you own a company which pays a dividend to your personal bank account (through a correspondent bank), and you subsequently buy stocks. This transaction is scrutinized by the sending bank, the correspondent bank, the receiving bank, and the stock broker. And it can be frozen at every step. Believe me: I *had* accounts and payments frozen at every step of this chain. Yes, this is a waste of energy and money. And yes, you pay for all this through fees.

It's out of control. I compare it to piss-testing for doping at every amateur football level from children to adults, everywhere in the world, every match and training. It's an invasion of privacy and human dignity. And it's not just banks. Accountants, public notaries, agents, and anybody else with a license is forced into unpaid policing. And this avalanche of data doesn't even result in money launderers being convicted. Take for example the traditional banking system of the US, where according to a Justice Department's prosecutor, 99.9% of cases remain unprosecuted.[75]

9.4 Control Your Profile

It does not take a genius to see where this is going. More national and international databases are linked all the time, combing everything from public and private sources. There's no escaping this. Staying out of every database in the world in and of itself could make you a suspicious undocumented character. Ideally, you put some thought into what information you want in these databases.

Yes, ironically being in the computers can be both necessary and beneficial for you. Try being consistent and the least suspicious as possible. Be a boring, repetitive person in the databases. Pay with cash where still possible. Cash is still king in a large part of the world. This way you prevent your entire life from being data-mined and sold to anyone with deep enough pockets or a few stripes on their arms. They want information. It's in your best interest to match a typical profile. Where do bureaucrats get their information? From you! Think about this when you fill out a form, download an app, or swipe a card.

9.5 How to Prevent Being Flagged as "Suspicious?"

Don't get scared. Ninety-nine percent of transactions go through as intended. But as mentioned, a CI can be flagged based on international transfers, living habits, or exotic sources of income.

Luckily, there are a few things you can do to not raise suspicion. Try blending in. Think about what your old, normie neighbors are doing. Next are tactics for smooth access to financial services:

- Consistency. Try to be typical, and consistent. Bean counters love consistency, and recurring payments are rarely scrutinized. Monthly salaries. Recurring income. Quarterly dividends. Those are all logical payments.
- The above is even truer when buying and selling crypto. Create a system, and stick to what works. And unlike peer-to-peer systems, you cannot wire "your money" wherever you want (hint: money deposited in a bank is no longer yours. You just become a creditor to the bank. That's why your account is "credited" and not "asseted").
- Don't use your accounts to receive payments from unknown sources, which are instantly sent to a third party. This is a major red flag because it can be used as a way to hide the original source of funds, a crucial aspect of money laundering.
- Certain countries are considered high risk, as are particular activities such as gambling or porn, and crypto-currency activities. Buying

Bitcoin or sending money to Somalia with the wrong bank account results in instant closure.

- Use accounts for specific functions. One for savings and investments while another is used to receive salary or payments. Try to be consistent with each in what goes in and out.

- Transactions from one bank account in your own name to another (even abroad) raise less suspicion. There is, after all, no taxable event when transacting with yourself. You can use this to perhaps set up a local bank account in your name in the country of your clients and then transfer internationally to another account in your name.

- Some banks are not accustomed to buying cryptos or international transactions. For others, it's their core-business. Some are used to clients moving or spending money abroad, others are not. Your familiar local bank might be the worst solution.

- Do things in line with previous activities or at least the conditions under which the account was opened.

- Sudden fluctuations in amounts are red flag for banks. If for years you earn 1.5k per month and suddenly you receive 75k it will be noticed. Keep this in mind the next bull-run.

- Don't use tricks, or fake data. I had a client trying to use a known mailbox address as house address. This doesn't work (and hasn't for a while).

- Be careful how you login as your IP address is logged by banks. They can block access after logins from unrecognized countries. A VPN helps you stay consistent.

- Apply flag theory and common sense. If a bank or country is too difficult, look further. I opened an account in Asia and the bank agent asked me for the reason. I said: "ATM," and made a gesture of sticking an ATM card in the wall. That was it. For someone who worked his way through month long account opening processes, compliance approvals, and Enhanced Due Diligence procedures, it was a breath of fresh air!

9.6 Reasons for Opening Offshore Bank Accounts

I get it, you post on Reddit that you will hold on to Bitcoin until it becomes the monetary standard. My experience with the last significant bull run, however, is that CIs look for a place to store part of their wealth. I know people who left the space all together. Not everybody enjoys 20% daily swings and endless silly memes.

When it comes to banking, most stick to what they know. They trust their local bank more than foreign banks. This is even true in countries where the banking system already failed, such as Cyprus and Greece. Western banks are too leveraged; they have lent out 10, 20, sometimes 50 times the amount of funds they have in deposit.

Governments in the Western world have guaranteed an amount of funds in case a bank goes bankrupt. Now, depositors don't have an incentive to research what a bank is doing with their money because they think their accounts are safe. Banks take risks because they know they can get away with it (moral hazard).[76] And the biggest joke: there aren't enough funds available in case a serious crisis hits. It's just a promise of the government (=worth nothing). The banks in your country are not as safe as you think.

Here are other reasons for opening an offshore bank account.

- Greater privacy – real bank secrecy is all but dead, especially for the tax man. But you can still protect from the public and prevent your financial data from being mined and sold by using reputable (smaller) banks in solid jurisdictions.
- Easier account opening procedures and less regulation – Banks can be a nightmare to open accounts in terms of paperwork. However, places exist where it can be done with a passport and a smile.
- Lower banking charges – If a low cost bank for (international) transactions and account maintenance isn't found in your country, you might find a better option offshore.

- Exchanging cryptos – if you live in a country where banks don't allow transactions with known exchanges, you might be able to open an account in a country that does.

- To protect against political oppression, financial instability, or other nonsense such as social credit-scores or sustainability points.

- Currency risk – If your national currency has a tendency to hyper-inflate, a bank account in a stable currency is essential.

- Capital controls – I had a client from Morocco living in the UK who told me his government made it so hard for money to leave the country it was easier for his father to take out cash, exchange it on the black market and fly to the UK to hand it over in person. For them, a foreign bank account means less headaches. I had clients from Argentina, Greece, and Venezuela with similar stories. Mandatory exchange rates, capital controls, and other nonsense "for the common good" aren't what a self-respecting CI subjects himself to.

Reasons NOT to open a foreign bank account: tax evasion and privacy from government.

9.7   Insider Tips for Opening Bank Accounts

Opening bank accounts in general is becoming cumbersome and bureaucratic. Having overseen maybe 50 corporate bank account opening meetings and many more paper applications, I think I have unique insights into the process.

First, you cannot walk into a random branch and expect to open an account. Regular staff only help regular customers. International customers are handled by specialized departments. This is especially true for banks in financial centers such as Switzerland, Hong Kong, Singapore, and Dubai. These banks only accept customers introduced by verified agents, and they want to meet you in person. In such cases, you should hire an agent offering "bank introduction" services. This is the quickest way to talk to the right person. It doesn't always have to be a paid service. Sometimes, asking around with visa or real estate agents can get you to the right person. Expat forums are an interesting source of information. Google "open a bank account in ... (wherever you are)" is a neat first step.

For personal banking it might be an idea to look beyond well-trodden paths. Most agents promote banks in offshore financial centers, but they are all under scrutiny. While it's difficult to open an account in typical offshore banks, it can still be easy to open an account in a "local" bank in a non-suspicious jurisdiction. It's frequently thought that one needs to be a resident in order to open a bank account, but flexible banks ask as little as a passport copy. Moreover, they less strictly enforce KYC rules since they aren't subject to intense monitoring, and they know the average person isn't a criminal.

When setting up a bank account for an offshore corporation use an agent. The first step is to setup the company, whereas the company opens the account. In order to do that, the company needs to pass a resolution. The agent has the template. This decision might need to be notarized, or even apostilled for international use. Sometimes, the agent can certify the signature on behalf of the bank.

When all documents are ready you can "meet" the bank. It has to be done in person, or online using Skype. Ideally, the agent gets informal approval or at least has an idea if your business is acceptable before you start collecting paperwork. You usually meet account managers at the bank. They're not the ultimate authority on deciding if your account gets approved.: that is "compliance." If the representative understands your case, it's easy for him to present it to compliance. Imagine a humpbacked, drooling compliance officer kept in the basement who needs to understand your business in five seconds. The better the information, the easier the process. It is smart to make an overview on how the account is going to be used.

Compliance approves a case as presented. When your case changes (adding a new currency or signatory, or the transacted volumes are higher than approved), you might need additional approvals. Make sure your case is as clear as possible from the start. After approval, you receive your account details. Before you get the internet token or a banking pass, you usually need to fund the account with a minimum account deposit. Only then will you have full access.

9.8   What Do Banks Want?

When opening a bank account, you run into paperwork. Here I explain what is needed and why. The following is usually required for the signatory of the account and of others in the structure (shareholders, directors, UBOs) in case of a corporate account.

9.8.1   Utility bill

Banks almost always ask for an up to date utility bill in your personal name. This should be a "consumption bill," demonstrating the use of utilities at the mentioned address. Examples are bills for electricity, water, gas, a telephone land line (not mobile), and internet connections. In certain cases, extracts from government registrations, rental contracts, title deeds, or bank statements can be used. They cannot be older than three months. You need this, there are no excuses.

For the bank, this proves where you live. It tells them if there's a risk of tax evasion, and if you're subject to automatic exchange of information obligations (CRS). It indicates where to send login details, banking tokens, or possible legal notices.

9.8.2   Tax Residency Certificate

While utility bills were enough in the past, financial institutions increasingly ask for more official confirmation of tax residency. This can be just a tax-number, or even a Tax Residency Certificate (TRC).

A TRC is an official document in which the government confirms you are a resident there. Governments don't hand this out easily and demand all kinds of evidence you were in fact living there. In some countries it is hard to get because of weird requirements or because they don't know what you are talking about. For now, this is not a widely requested document, but it seems to be heading in this direction.

9.8.3 Source of Funds Report

Banks have to understand what your business is. With an existing account they can figure this out by looking at your transactions. But when you open an account, they are in the dark. That's why they always ask their clients for the initial source of funds, a list of transactions and expected income, and what is the expected frequency and volume.

This gives the bank an indication as to the size and nature of your business and wealth (and if it matches your profile). Clients have often tried to skip through this process, presenting vague plans, and sometimes even get agitated stating they don't know yet. Imagine calling an airline to buy a ticket not knowing where you want to go or on which date. You have to give them something.

Unfortunately, due to the nature of crypto-currencies, a Source of Funds reports can be a hard requirement. There are banks in solid banking jurisdictions such as Liechtenstein and Switzerland that are willing to take on whales (and sometimes dolphins). However, they require a complete audit, not only of all material transactions and trades, but also of the source of the original funds used to buy the first coins. The "logic" being that they are required by law to ensure they aren't the final haven for illicit funds wired to them through cryptos.

Not everybody has the documents to prove their source of funds, and not everybody is willing to undergo privacy-sensitive procedures. Excessive coin-mixing and DeFi swaps could also close this avenue. Of course, there are always banks with less strict requirements. An alternative is to hold on to your coins until you can use them everywhere.

9.8.4 Your Resume

Banks don't care if you worked a summer as a bartender in Greece, whether you have perfect Excel capabilities, or your hobby is collecting stamps. They ask for CVs to verify your story. If you flipped burgers for a decade and suddenly propose to receive large payments from Bolivia, a bank might expect something fishy. This is an extreme example, but a resume does reveal who you are and what you're capable of. "Polishing" is easy to spot.

I was asked to register a company for two clients. One had finished a Ph.D. in his early 20s and did three masters afterwards. The other was working on a Master's Degree in Poland at the age of 18 while simultaneously running a business in Italy. These people were so eager to look respectable, they stuffed their CVs with unrealistic achievements. I found a few other strange things and suspected fake personalities. I checked later and their online profiles had disappeared. I think I was right to refuse them.

9.8.5 Reference Letter

Sometimes banks ask for reference letters before an account can be opened. These normally are letters from other banks to prove existing banking relations. This can be a problem; not all banks nowadays issue such letters. In fact, employees often don't even know what it is, and banking has become so impersonal that no one can vouch for you anymore.

Sometimes, it can be solved by providing six months' worth of bank statements, or letters from licensed professionals such as accountants or lawyers. I heard of a bank in Panama that asked for three reference letters. Despite their image, Panamanian banks have always been selective with opening bank accounts.

9.8.6 Passport Copy (of all the people involved)

Obviously, banks want to know who they're dealing with. You need a valid passport—there's no way around it. With remote account opening, this passport needs to be certified by the agent or notary. By the way, be mindful with your passport copy. Whenever you're asked for a passport copy (hotels, travel agencies, banks, etc.) write on it who made the copy and why. If you're asked for a scan, add a little note with the date and the organization you're scanning it for. This prevents your passport from being used for nefarious activities. You wouldn't believe what can be done with just your passport copy.

Nowadays a selfie with your passport or ID is a common requirement. Know that up until a couple of years ago, you had to go to a notary and have him certify a copy of the passport and send it around the world by courier. Nevertheless, remember the above: always include the date and organization it is for (or create a watermark in the image).

9.8.7   Additional Requirements

In addition, banks can ask for a:

- Copy of corporate documents, also of the shareholders (if applicable).
- Formal company decision to open the bank account (see "resolutions").
- Business plan.
- Minimum amount of turnover or a minimum deposit into the account.

These documents can be required to be in original form, translated to the language of the country of the bank, or notarized by a public notary.

9.8.8   Updated Bank Records

One of the downsides of regulations nowadays is the desperate need to comply. They would rather keep the authorities happy than you. Moreover, banks need to keep their records up-to-date. This can be annoying, especially when enforced by blocking transfers until you provide what they ask.

When your passport expires, they might ask for an updated copy. If you move, they'll want to see a recent utility bill. If your company has a corporate shareholder, they might ask if it is in good standing. The only way to prevent this from interfering with your business is to be proactive with updating these details yourself. Naturally, no one ever does this, but I thought I'd leave it here anyway.

9.9 Taking Credit-Card Payments

If you need to accept online payments other than crypto, your options in terms of where you can incorporate your company are limited. As difficult as it has become to open bank accounts, merchant accounts are far worse.

Those in the Western world don't understand how difficult it can be to accept online payments. I did a search into credit card processors and noticed that roughly 95% of them served the US and 80+% served the rest of the Western world. About 40% also served Hong Kong and Singapore. Outside of these core blocks, things are difficult, especially as far as traditional offshore companies are concerned. From a tax perspective, fiscally transparent entities[77] in the US or Europe are an option but need careful planning to work. Otherwise, low tax options in Europe are the way to go.

Corporate accounts at Stripe and PayPal are available in limited places, they need the corporation and its bank account to be in the same jurisdiction, and they sometimes require substance such as proof of a company address. You could use your personal Paypal account on behalf of the company, but this is best done in a low-tax environment or when just starting out.

There are specialist credit card processors working specifically with high-risk businesses and offshore companies. Unfortunately, they often require significant history and turnover, which starters don't have. Don't be discouraged though, there are always options.

Also, don't assume that with non-banks no reporting goes on. PayPal has a PDF of sixty pages with organizations they share your information with.[78] My interpretation: they cooperate with any government (without questions), and they sell your data to everyone willing to pay for it.

9.10 Welcoming Crypto Payments

It is an attack on liberty when you have to now beg big faceless corporations to use their monopoly on payments. Luckily, Bitcoin cuts out the middleman completely! I hope cryptos replace government issued fiat shit-coins, and I think Bitcoin remains the most used crypto. It has the network effect, the strongest security, the best development process, it is fully decentralized, and it has a massive ecosystem build around it.

Unparalleled benefits determine why Bitcoin is far superior to credit-cards. First of all, you are 100% in control. It is a peer-to-peer payment system, meaning you deal directly with the buyer and paying can be as easy as sending a Whatsapp message. Secondly, accepting payments is as easy as installing a piece of software; no need to file forms or go through compliance approvals. There are no monthly subscriptions costs or conversion fees, and the transactions fees are super low (see below). Next, you don't have to deal with third parties, and there are no geographical restrictions.

As of now, there are a few downsides: the price of Bitcoin is still volatile. It is awesome when you receive a payment and the next week it is worth 10% more; it feels far more terrible when it lost 10%. This also makes bookkeeping difficult. As of now, it isn't widely used outside of a few niche markets, although this is changing. Moreover, in certain countries, Bitcoin is outright banned.

The easiest method of accepting payments is by simply handing out your Bitcoin address. They can pay directly from their wallet to yours. This is not an automated system, however. To address this there are online payment systems connected to known Wordpress shopping carts. Here you can rely on third-party providers who charge a small fee (<1%). Alternatively, you become your own payment provider running your own node.[79] There are also providers that allow you to accept crypto payments, but pay you in USD.

In technology, it is common for additional layers to be built on existing technologies. An example is the internet, for which "ancient" protocols such as TCP/IP and DNS still function as the base-layer.[80] Likewise, exciting developments happen on the "second layer" of Bitcoin. One is called the Lightning Network. It allows you to make and receive instant global payments without middlemen that cost a fraction of a cent![81]

9.11 The Most Dangerous Number in Business

So far we discussed what you can do to prevent scrutiny. But nothing can be done when entire banks are frozen out of the system. An example is FBME Bank in Cyprus, which was accused (not convicted) of maintaining accounts used for money laundering and terrorist financing. The entire bank was cut from the financial system, affecting all the clients who never did anything wrong. We had a client with a successful company with a corporate bank account there he used for salaries, supplies, and billing clients. He tried opening an alternative bank account, but due to the changing regulatory environment this proved to be difficult. His business slowly died in front of his eyes.

This all boils down to the most dangerous number in business: one. This could have been prevented if the company had two bank accounts, preferably in two jurisdictions. If something happens to one, you're still in business with the other. It might be an idea to have multiple credit card processors, sell in multiple (crypto) currencies, and sell in diverse markets and countries. If anything fails, it won't impact you. The same goes for ATM cards, wallets, file storage systems, phones, emails, etc.

10. <Asset Haven – 4th Flag_

At the end of 2017, I received an email from a Canadian entrepreneur who was doing consultancy work in Africa. He was making good money, but he worried about his financial future. This was mainly due to his parents, who wanted him to buy a house in Vancouver before he was forever priced out of the market. In addition, they argued he needed to be in the social security system and contribute to a safe government pension. He wasn't asking for my opinion on this matter, but rather how to do it tax efficiently. I gave him my opinion anyway. I told him Vancouver real estate was one of the biggest bubbles in the world and to assume prices would rise for another few decades was foolish. Additionally, social security is an empty promise and pension-funds are a gigantic sucking black-hole and reason enough for immigration.[82] Needless to say, I never heard from him again.

This little episode made me realize my views differ from what is mainstream. What it revealed to me is how the concept of "wealth protection" is perceived. As a CI you move into the free market, but in my generation nobody knows what this means. As an international CI, there is no government to support you in ill health or old age. You alone are responsible for your financial future!

10.1 Ploys of the Filthy Rich

One of the biggest misconceptions about wealth is that it sits in the hands of "filthy rich," who once wealthy sit back, deposit their funds in an offshore trust, and live on interest for generations to come. The truth is different.

Wealth is an elusive companion. It can go as fast as it came. If a time-line is long enough, all fortunes evaporate.

Test this. Pick a list of rich folks, such as Forbes, and compare it with the list from one year ago. You'll see major moves up and down the list. But now take one from ten years ago, you'll see completely different names. If you look at a list from 100 years ago, the names are unfamiliar. Think of the long list of the rich and famous who lost everything—*often to great amusement of the general public.*

Keeping wealth is even more difficult than building it. It demands skills few possess, such as discipline, diligence, and patience. This is the exact opposite to what makes one successful in business and trading, such as quick decision making and risk taking. Moreover, few wealthy individuals are able to pass money skills on to their children. In fact, transferring wealth to children is a major concern of rich people, especially when little Johnny lacks the skills and discipline of a wealth builder, but has the spending habits of one. No wonder variations of the expression *"shirt sleeves to shirt sleeves in three generations"* exists in cultures around the world.[83]

It's not easy to keep wealth intact. The world is ever changing, and allocating a large pool of capital is difficult. There are fees, taxes, currency conversions, and transaction costs to consider. Wealth has to grow, or it diminishes. To grow, it has to incur risk. In the search for returns, people make the wrong investment decisions all the time. They can have bad luck or adopt excellent advice which turns out to be wrong.

I cannot tell you how to successfully manage wealth (I am not wealthy), but I do know a thing or two about the common risks and the legal protection from them. Don't assume this advice only applies to billionaires. Remember, rich people are nothing but you thirty years from now. Ambitious and hardworking CIs have a favorable chance to one day own at least a house or other assets. The pitfalls are the same. Wealth is attacked from all sides by governments, economic turmoil, business failures, lawsuits, failed marriages, disease, and criminals. And it'll only get worse in this age of transparency and revitalized Marxism.

10.2   The Mindset of the Global Wealth Builder

Imagine your holdings go to the moon. It is pointless to keep all your wealth in crypto. How to store it somewhere safe? Applying flag theory, you look for jurisdictions with respect for private property, strong asset protection laws, a healthy economy, and a sane and free market-oriented government with little debt. They have to score highly on respect for privacy, communications, professionalism, and stability.

Such qualifications are not static. Single countries can move in the direction of financial freedom to oppression and back. This is the reason why capital mobilizes the moment and things take a turn for the worse. Attempts to redistribute the wealth, usually redistribute the wealthy. The week Francois Hollande announced a 75% income tax on wealthy individuals, I received three calls from French guys wanting to move to Dubai.

With the earliest signs of socialism, you reevaluate the safety of your assets. Radical economic reforms such as price controls, exchange controls, investment restrictions, and laws which forbid citizens from owning foreign assets are the writing on the wall. From September 2019 onwards, I saw a spike in Lebanese trying to pull their money out of Lebanese banks and bringing it offshore (Dubai and Cyprus). The majority of clients, evidently, only found out the banks were insolvent when in March 2020 they lost access to "their" money.

Calls for taxes on the rich are another warning sign, especially because "the rich" is not a well-defined concept. In communist Cambodia, after all the rich had fled, been killed, or integrated into the new system, the anger simply transferred to those with signs of richness, such as having white skin, being able to speak French or English, or wearing glasses. You can go to the Killing Fields and see what's left of them and their children, including strings of hair, pieces of bone and broken toys.

Ideally, you stash your nest-eggs in Asset Havens away from where you're a citizen, a legal resident, or where you spend most of the time (the places you incur risks). Places such as Switzerland, Panama, the UAE, and Singapore have a superb track-record of safeguarding deposits, even in times of turmoil. Even when you don't move abroad, you can apply this principle. You're free to store your wealth in another jurisdiction, as long as you are transparent to the authorities (if required).

10.3   Next Level Hodling: International Assets

For those living and working in one place, their assets are at risk. It can be surprisingly easy to have bank accounts or assets frozen. I know of cases where accounts were frozen after a dispute about an unpaid invoice. The claimant was incorrect, but the owner needed to prove it. In the meantime, they barely escaped bankruptcy. People have used this power out of resentment or to "get even" in their own twisted little mind. And let's not talk about the power governments and ex-wives have over assets.

The reason why this works is all parties are within the same jurisdiction. A judge can hear the case, and his decisions can have a direct effect. However, when your assets are in another jurisdiction, a court ruling cannot automatically be enforced. It needs to be recognized and enforced by foreign courts. This can be a surprisingly difficult process, especially when multiple languages, legal systems and procedures are involved. This is even more so when countries are not on friendly terms, or have no history of legal cooperation. Keep in mind, this is not a get out jail free card. Governments have ways to go after tax evaders and criminals, especially if you're from the US or Europe.

Having international assets creates three layers of defense. As a first, it's difficult for the suing party to go after what they don't know you own, in particular in places without public registries. Secondly, the actual process of enforcing a ruling abroad is difficult and brings additional costs. A local judge can even throw a case out in case it is incompatible with local law. And finally, the prospect of having to go after foreign assets can deter them from even trying.

Keep this in mind in business dealings. If ever you're dragged into a court case, you want to be sure a ruling in your favor can be enforced. You can achieve this by choosing a court and governing law in the jurisdiction of your contracting parties. On the other hand, certain legal systems are so corrupt and dysfunctional, you want to stay far away from them. Outcomes from court cases in the third world can be determined by who offers the judge most. Sometimes courts rule against foreigners by default. I even read that Belgium courts tend to rule against Dutch people (fatnecks). To prevent being sucked into such a swamp, you can include international arbitration clauses in your contracts. This way you benefit from a private court system offering fast and fair rulings directly enforceable in 156 countries.[84]

10.4 Keep Your Mouth SHUT!

I had a client who had found himself wealthy with crypto currencies and moved to the Philippines. He became a vocal part of the community, and he had ambitious plans for starting a nationwide crypto exchange. I warned him. One of my other clients living there had recently been robbed in his own house. Not only did they take his valuables, they also beat him to a pulp and left him for dead. Besides a long recovery back to health and not being able to work, he had significant problems with replacing his passport and all his bank cards.

Our generation has a psychological need to flaunt their success on social media. Such high profile activity can be a mistake. Telling the world how much you make is not only unnecessary, it can be dangerous. Everybody deep down knows stealing is bad, and criminals come up with all sorts of justifications for their crimes: moral-superiority, injustice, or what a white person did 300 years ago. Flaunting your wealth in front of locals is ill-advised, especially when they have minority complexes, jealousy, and resentment for getting involved with "their" women.

The worst of all motivators is a deep ingrained feeling of unfairness. Rich people are never profiled as hardworking, valuable, and honest members of society. Rather, they are described as "filthy," and somehow blamed as a causes for one's failure or that of society. Bragging how wealthy you are gives every criminal, lawyer, and tax inspector sufficient fuel to go after to you as a bull charges a matador. Think about Leonardo de Caprio in The Wolf of Wallstreet throwing 100 USD bills at the FBI from his yacht. Bad idea.

The first rule of keeping your money: keep your mouth shut! Start by not volunteering information about your wealth on social media. Next, treat every form as an inquiry into your Pornhub history. Write N/A when questions are too probing. Think about your image. Being thought of as a tenant, caretaker, or a poor relative of a wealthy absentee landlord is better than being widely known as a real estate mogul. Be a sales representative of your business, and not the vice president. If you have an "invisible" active business online, even better—*no one needs to know differently.*

If you buy assets on public record, perhaps use a corporation so your ownership doesn't show up on a simple internet search. Another common process is to use front or straw men. In the corporate service industry, these are called nominees. A nominee on paper fills a legal role in a company. They can become the director, the secretary, or even the shareholder of a company. They represent the company on paper while you run everything behind the scenes.

Some try to use nominee shareholders to hide from the tax man... Don't. Eventually, you need to transfer your funds out of the company which is a taxable event. You cannot simply wire the money to your personal bank account. I met an ordinary working professional in trouble because dad left them a Swiss bank account. And as mentioned, banks always ask for the UBO anyway (the man behind the scenes).

Nothing offers better protection than living a low profile existence and calling minimal attention to yourself. Darwin noted the most effective life forms evolved to blend in with their environment. Animals camouflaged by nature became invisible to predators and more likely to survive.[85] The key is to fit in with those around you. Try not to make enemies or create jealousies. Live comfortably, but not decadently. Don't flaunt your lack of regard for local morality. Be respectful of local customs. Fit in! Become a chameleon, adapting to all places and communities. Crime is often done by those who directly or indirectly know you, and it helps to be seen as one of the good guys and an uninteresting target.

As always, this has two sides: an obsession with privacy can be interpreted as if you have something to hide. Also, it might be needed to project a certain level of success in your business or your marriage market. Show what you need to show. Manage your profile, both offline and online.

10.5   Keep it Simple

I was contacted by a client in a "high-risk" business. He was determined to limit personal liability. He asked a legal advisor how to do it and he came up with a plan to setup a US operating company, owned by a UK Ltd, owned by a Singapore LTD, owned by BVI Trust. This would result in the setup of four legal entities, with four bank accounts, four times bookkeeping and four times annual fees. And all this to achieve limited liability. But only in unusual cases, such as fraud, the veil of limited liability can be pierced, and this rarely happens. Moreover, international diversification limits this risk even further. Using an offshore holding company should be enough in terms of asset protection. Using such an extremely complex structure only results in an administrative nightmare, and I doubt any bank would open an account for it.

The same logic applies to other forms of elaborate asset protection plans. For average CIs, having assets discretely and strategically stored around the world is enough from an asset protection point of view. I see the occasional person eager to "do it right" and set up a complete asset protection strategy, including trusts and foundations. Such structures always result in costs, practical problems (try opening a bank account for a trust or foundation nowadays), and potential legal issues due to the complex nature of these products. There are great reasons to use them but not for the average person. They are mostly promoted in the US, where suing each other is a national sport and those with (perceived) wealth are specifically targeted. In the rest of the world, it's less likely you need them. I dealt with a number of structures set-up out of a sense of adventure or in the interest of the agent, rather than real need or common sense. Keep it simple.

10.6   Sovereign Investments

As mentioned, I am not an investment advisor. However, I can talk about basic practical and tax aspects of asset classes, other than cryptos, that I think are interesting for CIs:

10.6.1 Impossible to Confiscate: Foreign Real Estate

A property in a foreign country is an interesting and secure investment. First of all, it offers a place to lay low which is practically impossible to confiscate by a foreign creditor. Information on ownership is usually not easily discovered, especially when outside of bean counter nations. It's a solid hedge against inflation and economic turmoil. Whatever happens, the property remains where it is, and it can be a way generate extra "passive" rental income. And let's not forget the possible capital gains, especially when an economy is booming.

As a downside, it can be difficult to find your way in foreign real estate. Stick around for a while to understand the market and the process. The legal system is unknown, and can restrict your owning property as a foreigner. Trying to manage real estate from abroad can be a pain in the ass without a reliable local service agent. Moreover, real estate can be illiquid, meaning difficult to sell if you ever need to. I have a friend who bought a large estate in the Philippines on an impulse and hasn't been able to sell it for decades.

Real estate is almost always taxed in the country where it's situated. This includes rental income, capital gains, and other taxes. The reason? They're obviously locally sourced.

10.6.2 Hard and Eternal: Precious Metals

I am a bit of a gold / silver bug, and perhaps biased. But it's relatively easy to store insured precious metals in vaults in stable countries (allocated and registered in your name). You can even visit it or have it sent to you by courier. A number of organizations provide this service, and storage fees are cheap. Moreover, this is a very liquid investment, offering the chance for significant profits once a bull market gets under way.

Many "Gold Bugs" don't trust the financial system, and they want to hold precious metals in their hands. As a traveler this is difficult. I base this opinion on crossing borders with a few kilos of silver. It lights up the luggage scanner like a spot-light, and I ended up in the office of a charming Arab female police chief. She was interested in hearing about the coins, but didn't know what else to do with me and let me in. This was Dubai. I don't know how this process would go in a country in crisis or where this metal is worth more than the customs agent's annual salary.

Don't get caught up in the gold vs crypto debates (or in any other debates for that matter). There are times and use-cases for both. What is vital is that you protect yourself from out of control governments and central banks and precious metals can be a great tool in your arsenal. As long as you don't lose them in a boating accident...

10.6.3 Portable and Subtle: Intellectual Property

"Online real estate" is another interesting investment for CIs to pursue. These are digital products which can be sold / rented / licensed / advertised on. You can think about websites, apps, software, books, pictures, videos, and music. In short: everything being read, watched, listened, or used. You don't need a physical location and can manage everything from your laptop. It's perfect for those who wish to stay mobile and sovereign.

This strategy is possible for investment because you can pay developers / writers / marketers for creating products and systems to generate cash. If you don't have the money to invest, you can build products on your own. I pursued this strategy and it's paying off. Websites, books, training programs. Each income stream, no matter how small, makes your life a little easier. And, if what you create goes viral, it all goes into your pocket.

From a tax perspective, passive income is treated differently than active income, primarily due to interpretations of the "source." If it's foreign sourced income, it offers you ample possibilities for tax planning. On the other hand, various forms of passive income are taxed in the countries from which it's sourced. For example, the US taxes royalties (and other passive income) sourced in the US at 30%. As a result, income from sales on Amazon or the Appstore are often subjected to taxes (unless a tax treaty can be applied).

This kind of income is recurring, and incoming payments come from well-known brand names in first world countries. It's unlikely to cause you banking troubles. And what is the biggest risk when you advertise on a website or sell a book? A refund? A negative review? This low risk business activity doesn't require complicated legal structures. One real issue if you're using big publishers is censorship. This does happen more and more.

To create value you first figure out what people are actively looking for and come up with an elegant solution. The internet is a graveyard of brilliant ideas nobody cared about. Always let the market decide what product you create (ask your potential customers what they want), especially as a beginner entrepreneur. Trust me, I once wasted six months of my life creating a website nobody visited promoting a book nobody read.

10.6.4 Skills, Reputation, Network, and Knowledge

Invest in yourself. Think about paying for training, courses, qualifications, or experience by trial and error. Go broad or dive deep. Marvelous value can be created when combining two skills in a novel way. Think about directly sellable skills such as coding and online marketing, or skills that help you indirectly, such as presenting, philosophy, and entrepreneurship. Expand your mind with cooking, dancing, music, meditation, or yoga. Increase your confidence and stamina with martial arts. Explore the world on your own and discover yourself.

Having a wide variety of marketable skills, an international circle of connections, and multiple personally-owned businesses offer you the flexibility to see and exploit opportunities. These are all factors contributing to your happiness, prosperity, and safety. Moreover, you'll be confident and able to survive anywhere in the world. Become the mythical hydra monster: one head chopped off, two fresh ones arising from the stump.

Whenever I'm in an unfamiliar city, I notice that a fellow tourist, who has been there for one or two days, is a wealth of information on prices, where to go, how to get there, and what to look out for. He doesn't need to be a tour-guide with twenty years of experience to reveal valuable information! This applies to business as well. Where can you be of value?

As a CI, it's easy to connect to other crypto-enthusiasts and create an online tribe. Moreover, you possess interesting skills that can help others propel projects into the future. You can use these assets for interesting projects and benefit your fellow man.

10.7 Own Nothing, Control Everything

The apex of asset protection is to own assets through a trust or foundation. With this tactic, you legally no longer own these assets. The management of them is in the hands of professionals. You can indicate what needs to be done with those assets by sending a "letter of wishes," but the final decision on distribution of funds is with the trustee, or the foundation council. In practice those managing a trust or foundation are lenient towards the original owner of the assets. But I have seen cases where a trustee no longer entertained the wishes of a second generation beneficiary if they contradicted the original goals of the trust.

These arrangements should have a permanent nature to withstand legal scrutiny. A trust or foundation must be "irrevocable": meaning you truly entrust your life-savings to a third party. You're no longer an owner but a beneficiary. And the trust or foundation independently decides how the future of the estate is managed. You cannot undo this. So why would you want this? Let's look at a number of benefits:

1. Tax Benefits – A trust or foundation in a tax haven accumulates income without you having to pay income tax. After all, you cannot pay taxes on what you don't own. In certain cases, this can help avoid inheritance taxes, since technically ownership doesn't transfer to your children (no taxable event). One gigantic BUT: in countries such as the Netherlands and Canada, these structures can be considered fiscally transparent, and taxed as if still owned by the original owner. In addition, the increasing amount of General Anti Abuse Rules stipulate substance for trusts or foundations as well. Careful planning is needed, especially when assets in multiple jurisdictions are involved.

2. Protection from Lawsuits – If you were solvent the moment you transferred assets to the trust or foundation, you make it impossible for future creditors to touch the assets. You discourage anyone to

think about suing you because it doesn't have an effect on assets you legally don't own.

3. Estate Planning – Trusts or foundations can survive you, and you can appoint the beneficiaries for after you die. In Western countries, your heritage is divided according to the local law in order to make sure everybody gets a "fair share"—including the State, and perhaps family members you consider unworthy. If you have other ideas with your life's work, you can use an offshore trust or a foundation. If set up right, you can build a strong offshore flag supporting your family for generations to come. As mentioned above and depending on the circumstances, a trust or foundation might not eliminate taxes.

While all this sounds interesting, I always advise taking one step back when desiring a trust or foundation for asset protection and ask: protection from what? If you're an average CI doing business through a corporation, and you don't live in a sue-happy place, you aren't at much risk from lawsuits. If you would be, having international assets is already a large deterrent and a first barrier of defense.

In my opinion, setting up a trust or foundation should only be done with a strict goal in mind: tax planning, preventing potential family disputes, creating an umbrella for international assets, or managing a large estate over time. After all, there are annual returning costs associated with the structure as well as legal and privacy risks (Panama Papers).

In addition, a structure should be able to withstand the type of scrutiny you might expect, whether tax or legal challenges. A trust is a creature of common law and perhaps best used there. A foundation is a type of legal entity originated in civil law, and the logical option when protecting assets in civil law countries. Both have their benefits, downsides, and ideal use cases. This is not a do-it-yourself area.

Besides measurable goals (kids to college, use of your house), be realistic about what your wealth can do without you. Your estate might morph into something you never wanted. Your lawyer might be on the same page, but his replacement doesn't know you and isn't interested in conserving and distributing your wealth with minimum charges and taxes. Unfortunately, it is in their financial interest to maximize problems and litigation procedures. As if this is not enough, your children could party away the money or get caught up in a cult or religious movement. Your agreeable wife is just as agreeable when her brother calls for campaign contributions to get him elected for the People's Representative Council in Indonesia so he can fill his pockets with bribes to support the social media image of his plastic wife.

10.8 Building a Fortress against Scammers

I am often asked for advice about crypto investments. These are usually inexperienced investors who ran into an "opportunity." They have read about an amazing new coin but wonder if it is a scam. More often than not, they've already invested and are trying to get their "investment" back. It goes somewhat like this:

> *"Hey Wes, I've found this new XYZ coin. It is a new way of doing XYZ and it's going to revolutionize the world. What do you think?"*

Since this happens a few times each year, I've developed a few routine questions. Usually, it takes me a couple of minutes to figure out if it's a scam or not. I might not even have to look at the website. Other scams are setup quite well and require a deeper look (but never too deep).

Look, these schemes can sound legit and convincing. They push the right buttons. And because investments are a private aspect of life, you don't always hear about it when someone invested—*especially when it went wrong*. But believe me, they are everywhere! I have had the same discussion with my 60-year-old Dutch aunt, ex-girlfriends (and their friends) in Asia, my closest circle of high-school friends, my far away friends, colleagues, members of social clubs, etc.

Don't think you'll never fall for a scam. Bernie Madoff ran a pyramid scheme based on the principles set forth in this chapter for decades, selling to professional money-managers on Wall Street.[86]

Luckily, investment scams display common patterns. I have written them down so you can spot them in the future. Hopefully it'll save you money. But before we do that, let me define the two most common crypto-currency scams: pyramid schemes and high-yield exit scams.

10.8.1 The Long Term Con: Pyramid Schemes

With a pyramid scheme you, the investor, is promised a high return by investing into a (new) profit generating system. In order for you to be successful, you are encouraged to get your friends involved. Pyramid schemes are often sold as network marketing opportunities. However, with network marketing, a network is created to sell an actual (physical) product. With a pyramid scheme, you are the product.

Pyramid schemes often yield large returns in the beginning, but what investors often don't fully understand is that these returns are paid by the new participants (attracted by the high returns). The system works until no new investors can be found. Then it collapses, and participants realize what they invested in the system is gone.

10.8.2 The Houdini Act: High Yield Investment Schemes

High Yield Investment Schemes have many variations, but their goal is for you to throw money in opportunities that are too good to be true. The sales techniques used for these types of schemes are similar to those used for pyramid schemes. But while a pyramid scheme thrives by large numbers of small investors over longer periods of time, a HYIS focuses on selling high-ticket investments as fast as possible and disappearing with the money.

It's difficult to stop such scams, since from the outside it's not always verifiable that what is being sold has no value. I attended an "entrepreneur boot camp" where they convinced housewives to go 16.000 EUR into debt to buy a foreign exchange currency trading course to make "thousands of dollars a month from home." In theory it's possible, but it will never work in practice.

10.8.3 How to Recognize Crypto-Currency Scams

Now that we know the common scams, let's look at how to recognize them. As mentioned, they often push the same buttons to convince you to join.

Vague products

A common feature of scams is that the specifics on how the investment works remain vague. Examples are "automated coin trading software," "coin trading software," "secret systems normally only used on Wall Street," "revolutionary new block chain application," or a "unique new method for tokenizing the world."

A vague investment is better: it enhances the mystery, tickles the fantasy, and obscures what's going on. You'll find that "investors" cannot explain how the money is made—*how the value is created.* All they see is the wave of money about to flood in...

Investment "Packages"

Another common theme, especially with pyramids, is investment "packages," such as bronze, silver, and gold. The more you put in, the higher your return. In addition, there are incentives for "re-investing" the earnings. The ultimate goal is to keep money in the system and let nothing out.

Poor Structure

The people behind scams are usually salesmen without an understanding of the frameworks real businesses work upon. The way a scam is set up and legally structured always reveals cracks upon closer inspection.

One time, I analyzed an "automatic trading system" profiting from the bull market in gold. However, the bull market had ended two years before! The company claimed it sold gold in Germany and had registered for VAT. But the type of product sold was VAT exempt in Germany. Finally, it claimed it had an office registered as FANCY NAME LIMITED in the Dubai Multi Commodities Free Zone. But to trade gold there, you need a special license and a company ending with "DMCC," not "Limited." I know this because I lived in this free zone and my job was registering such entities.

You might wonder: why invest in a bubble that's already burst? But then you underestimate the power of investment scams. Often people have no clue what they invest in anyway. They see friends make money and want a shortcut to the same result.

Unrealistic Investment Returns

Scams are attractive because they offer extremely high returns, such as 1% a day, or 20% a month. Beginning investors have difficulties understanding how unrealistic this is. They don't understand exponential growth.

Allow me to explain it with an example:

If you invest 1.000 USD for a return of 20% a month, after 1 month you have 1.200 USD (+200). After two months, you have 1.200 + 20% = 1.440 (+240). After three months, you have 1.440 + 20% = 1.728 (+288).

As you see, the invested amount doesn't increase in a straight line. Every month it grows exponentially bigger. It starts off slow, but goes parabolic fast!

After 12 months, you're almost at 9.000 USD, and after 24 months it's almost 80k. And yes, after 38 months, you're a millionaire.

Question: do you think someone who created a revolutionary system with which he could grow one thousand USD to one million in little over three years needs your investment? Of course not.

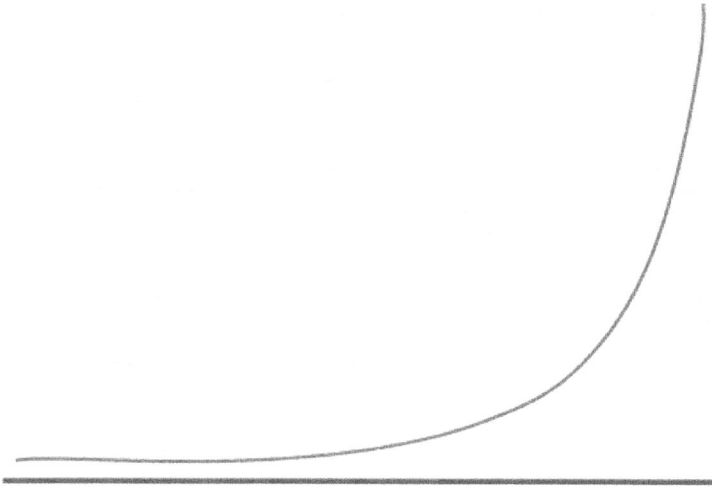

Our revolutionary trading system can turn 1.000 USD into 1.000.000 in little over three years. Instead of using it to become rich, we want you to give us your money and ask your friends to do the same.

You're the Product

Since no actual product is sold, the marketing of investment scams focuses on the investor... You!

They move the discussion away from the technical details by painting a picture of massive future prosperity. A life of excitement, adventures, traveling, parties, expensive cars, and wild women. Instantly transform a struggling existence into a life of the rich.

Advanced scams include training programs, mind-mapping, aligning with the universe, getting rid of scarcity mind-set, and other bullshit. They prepare you for your-soon-to-be-found riches, even going as far as having you imagine the houses you'll own and charities you'll support. After all, with great wealth comes great responsibility!

And remember: no work is needed, and it happens overnight!

Social Proof

The main reason investment scams are effective is because of something called "social proof." Again, this can take a variety of shapes. The standard pyramid relies fully on fresh blood, and there are rewards for bringing in friends and for being vocal on social media. I have even seen the use of paid actors standing up in the crowd as living testimonials. Everything to spread the word—*and spread it fast.*

More advanced scams target trusted advisors, celebrities, or other opinion makers to get to their followers. This can be done by convincing them directly, falsely using their name, or using what they said out of context. As of late, scammers hack the Twitter accounts of celebrities and ask their followers to send over coins, promising to return double the amount they receive.

Having a regular Joe make money is a super effective way to lower someone's defenses, since it demonstrates that "it works." Moreover, if someone close to you is convinced, it becomes difficult to resist when they made "all this money" for months. Moreover, not believing the scam equates to saying the friend cannot be trusted.

This makes talking about the subject delicate. You'll often find that not only are you dealing with the person you talk to, but also their devoted best friend or lover in the background. You can come up with logic and reason, but they are hooked emotionally. It doesn't matter what you say if they "feel" the opposite. And few readily admit (financial) mistakes. And then there are those who refuse to believe they were scammed long after they lost their investments and the promoter is in chains.

The Best Salesmen in Town

Those promoting investment scams usually drank the cool-aid themselves. Early investors in scams become religious defenders, unable to stop talking about their sudden riches. The evidence is right there on their Youtube channel. They went from nobody, who used their first "profits" to buy a new webcam, to five months later being invited to parties in Thailand where Lamborghini's are given away.

If a promoter is sufficiently high or early in a pyramid, they've helped others achieve financial success as well. This total devotion makes them such effective salesmen; they 100% believe it and have the track record! Even when deep down they know something is fishy, they see the daily profits for themselves and those around them. Friends sent them letters thanking them for changing their lives—*it's hard to stay rational in this situation.*

I had friends who invested in a scam, fully aware it was a pyramid scheme. It started rationally, but at one point their words changed, and they were going to make 100k USD a year by "pumping" their profits back in. Shortly after, the bubble popped and we didn't hear about it anymore.

Legal Blowback

Investment scams are not only a way to lose money, but they can also have legal repercussions. In Western countries, there is experience with pyramid schemes, and governments are (a little) active in tackling them.

Developing countries are wising up also. And for good reason. Asia is especially a haven for this stuff. It has a growing middle class which suddenly has money to spend. Moreover, people in this area of the world are social media addicts, have no previous experience with investing, and extremely sensitive to what friends and family do.

Pyramid schemes violate securities laws in countries around the world, especially without proper registration or a license to solicit investments from the public. Look, I am not naively saying that something "regulated" cannot be a scam. In fact, I've seen it being used as a sales argument.

Nevertheless, it's quite a large legal dragnet a promoter can get tangled in, and they often end up with legal problems.[87] This can include you if have been raving about the scheme on social media. Sometimes, when it comes to legal matters, victims are contacted for funds to start a legal recovery action against the original scammer. The victims who were burned once, are scammed again. After all, they already proved to be the ideal group to approach!

And that's not all. Promoting scams can reflect terribly on your social life, especially when your friends lost money through your recommendations. And not all investors call the police. A crowd of angry investors in South Africa set the house and cars of a promoter of a pyramid scam ablaze. And an angry investor in an investment scam in Dubai real estate resorted to cutting the promoter's fingers off in an effort to get his money back.

11.   <Playgrounds – 5th Flag_

You might be wondering what to do with all your low-tax income. Well, spend it on living an epic life! The world is your playground. Think about your dream destination. Envision a marvelous journey. Get out there. Experience wild and epic adventures. Enjoy yourself by partying the night away in Latin America, diving in the red sea, having an awesome safari in Tanzania, or doing charity work in Africa.

11.1   Work Hard, Play Hard

The term "playgrounds" is a broad definition, a canvas you can paint your future on. It is roughly defined by the countries where you like to spend your time. Where can you do what you want without breaking laws or upsetting the locals? Quality of life should be your top priority. Countries awash with tourists would be a wonderful start; all facilities are there, and you blend in.

Don't mix it up. Countries interesting from a living point of view can be too dysfunctional or instable to plant other flags. You might want to spend time in Cuba if you enjoy dancing salsa, but you'd never invest your pension in Havana real estate. A CI always stays informed on political changes and avoids countries with a history of socialism and confiscating private assets.

Ideally, none of your assets are located in these playgrounds, and none of your passports or other paperwork are issued by them. Playgrounds are those places where it's safe for you to relax and enjoy life. The local government should see you as a temporary tourist supporting the local economy.

Stay informed on how long one may stay without being considered a resident for tax purposes. For this reason, it might be necessary to have two, three, or four playgrounds. Tax planning might allow you to spend all of your time in one playground. For a CI, it's safest to avoid spending more than 90 days per year in any particular country.

Even popular destinations have bad seasons. Thailand has a rainy and a burning season. Bali has a rainy season when the waves are shit. Northern Europe can be too cold in winter and Southern Europe too hot in summer. Consider these factors and remember you're free to go anywhere!

11.2   Living the Good Life

One of the nicest parts of being a CI is the annual review of what the world has to offer, followed by a decision on what to try next. Are you going for outdoor life and sports, exploring nightlife, food and culture, or relaxing in nature? A CI constantly lives in the type of environment or climate he desires. Want an eternal spring and to never see snow again? You can. Want to spend the rest of your days surfing the best waves or skiing down the best slopes, you can do that too!

Traveling broadens horizons and educates minds. It's the ultimate growth experience. It enables you to see and understand matters beyond the comprehension of those who stay at home. You don't have to travel constantly; you can do as Tim Ferris suggested and take mini retirements: work three months and make an epic journey of a month to a special place.

Playgrounds don't require legal registration. Hold onto your status as a tourist. I'll admit, staying on tourist visas and doing visa runs (going in and out of the country to get a new visa) isn't always fun or easy. They are a puzzle and an art on their own, but worth it.

11.3   Settling Down in Paradise

My observation is that most CIs create a base. Traveling permanently is tiring, and having a favorite country is not a bad thing. You can still be free and have a higher standard of living than you're used to. Having your house cleaned is the norm in large part of the world, and drivers and servants are readily available. Become a patron of a worthy cause. Join clubs, get a social circle, and be a sparkling resident who allows everyone around him to flourish.

Be careful with expensive possessions that tie you down. Villas and apartments are often difficult to maintain or sell, and they should only be considered when truly settling down. They can be rented for the short term. Don't pursue luxurious toys such as cars, boats, and consumer goods unless you're passionate about them. They interfere with a mobile, international lifestyle. A CI needs to be ready to move on and let go of physical possessions if necessary. Keep your cost of living low. Spend little on expensive, depreciating things. This leads to greater accumulation of wealth and ultimately freedom.

A typical "mistake" I see is that when people enjoy living in a country they start mixing up all their flags in rapid fashion. They spot opportunities, surprised by why "someone isn't doing this?" They dump their savings in any number of opportunities. More often than not, they fail due to invisible hurdles and red tape. But even when successful, all sorts of dynamics come into play, especially when out-muscling local competition. Business grows. Your name is humming. The staff know the turnover you made. This is where trouble begins.

Be aware of the local culture. The Philippines is a great place for holidays or living a well-deserved retirement. But it can be a dangerous place. Foreigners are killed on occasion. Things get even trickier when you start to place your hands in local pockets, which is what a successful "foreigner" is perceived to be doing. I think the going price for an assassination was 15.000 pesos, which is about 300 USD. There are business men who would use it to get rid of a debt or a successful competitor.

In Cambodia, a Dutch entrepreneur wanted to fire an employee who was stealing. The employee warned him he couldn't be fired because of his social standing. He fired him anyway and was poisoned the same day. He only survived because the dosage used was not enough for a large Westerner. And in Fortaleza, Brazil, all the business men endured annoying vendors, massage ladies, and police men who didn't pay in their restaurants. If they spoke up, at night their businesses would be set ablaze.

Indonesia is far less dangerous, but from a business perspective it's treacherous. The folks here disregard legal arrangements. Landlords double the rent at the end of the year if they think the business is successful, or after the tenant himself made enhancements to the building. Or they let the same property to two tenants, and spend the money on religious ceremonies. A court case is decided based on who pays the biggest bribe. Expats have containers with furniture and personal belongs stalled at entry ports for an invented issue, and only released after a bribe is paid.

Westerners always underestimate how corrupt and dysfunctional the world is. Sometimes, the only reason people work in the government is to fill their pockets. Getting elected is an investment which has to be paid back by selling favors. Equality before the law is absent. You'll always be a foreigner, culturally and legally. If you overstay your visa, or behave in an undesirable way, you're thrown out or put in jail. Don't step on anyone's toes. Drop the Western "my rights" attitude.

Of course this is not conclusive advice. There are great opportunities out there and adventures to be had. Besides, achieving business success in a strange country can be highly rewarding. I had heaps of fun with my Filipina ex-girlfriend exploring all the business opportunities around us. Since then we broke up and now "death would be too good for me," so there's that.

Many before you have run businesses locally without trouble. As long as you act respectfully, don't get involved with the wrong crowds, or disregard social and moral codes, you should be fine. Perhaps team up with a local. See it as an experience. Mentally write off the cost. And don't bet your life on it; keep enough going offshore...

12. <Citizenship – 6th Flag_

Your passport is your most valuable possession if you wish to live the international high-life. Besides travel, it's needed for opening bank accounts and crypto exchanges or signing contracts with utilities.

Since a passport is essential, the government of the issuing country holds a certain amount of power over you. According to the early proponents of flag-theory, too much. To this day, second passports are a hot-topic. In my opinion, they are at the end of the list for the average CI. The real benefits you get from flag theory is when you start to factually internationalize your life. You need to start with that ASAP. A second passport is of secondary concern.

I observed that aspiring Flag Theorists use the investment of money and time needed for a second passport as an excuse to not do anything. Don't forget that a major reason passport programs are touted is because they are expensive and carry fat commissions.

Having said that, they can increase your freedom tremendously, and there are situations where a second passport is the first concern for living a respectable life.

12.1 Do You Need a Second Passport?

The person inspiring me to make the last jump as an international business man was an older Dutch gentleman who made the move himself in the 70s by moving to the Channel Islands. He has spent decades traveling the world while running a mobile business, first by phone and fax, and now by laptop. He told me he lived in Amsterdam at the start of World War II. One-hundred Jewish children were expelled from his school in 1941. After the war, only fifty-one returned. He has seen what it means to have the wrong identity. He is now using his wealth to invest in residency and passport programs for his staff. One of them is from the Philippines and is always having trouble traveling. Two other members of his team are Muslims from Sri Lanka. At the time of writing, Sri Lankan Muslims are having a hard time after a number of suicide attacks in 2019.[88] His efforts ensure these innocent families can always travel freely to flee prosecution or worse.

This example captures the group for which a second or new passports is most beneficial: oppressed groups, those from countries at war, and those at risk of bodily harm. I was told by a Cyprus citizenship agent that many Chinese clients want their family to get away from smog in China. Not strange, since in 2015 alone 1.8 million Chinese died due to pollution.[89]

Luckily, in the Western world we don't have such considerations. Having said this, there are those who could still benefit from a second passport. Let's not forget Edward Snowden and Julian Assange, who shed light on criminal activities of the government and cannot travel anymore. And of course there are the countless faceless men whose passports have been confiscated due to unpaid taxes, alimony, or political reasons. Imagine what this means for your dreams of having a nice life? A second passport, in some cases, can be a necessity.

With a second passport, you eliminate the disastrous effects such policies can have on you. First of all, you always have a place to go. Regardless of how bad things get, you'll have the right to live permanently in another country and possibly in several other countries (EU). Additionally, you may be extended special privileges and protections. Exciting new travel opportunities open up. Local banks open their doors and investments that were previously restricted, such as real estate, become available. Bottom line: you'll have more options, and thus more freedom.

12.2   What is Citizenship?

This definition comes from Encyclopedia Britannica:

> *Citizenship is the relationship between an individual and a State to which the individual owes allegiance and in turn is entitled to its protection. Citizenship implies the status of freedom with accompanying responsibilities. Citizens have certain rights, duties, and responsibilities that are denied or only partially extended to aliens and other noncitizens residing in a country.*[90]

The concept of citizenship is a narrower form of nationality, which can apply to boats, airplanes, and corporations. A The Hague Convention of 1930[91] defined the concept of nationality. It was agreed that each nation can determine under its own internal laws who are nationals. Each is free to decide to whom it grants nationality or citizenship, and from whom it may withdraw nationality. No State can force its nationality upon a foreigner who does not want it, and an individual can hold multiple citizenships (although not all countries allow it).

To some, citizenship is a mystic, quasi-religious concept. Challenging the wisdom of those in authority and the actions of the State is unpatriotic. For them, it might be upsetting to hear passports, citizenship, and places of residence are offered as business or convenience propositions. But frankly, aspiring residents and citizens look at countries as if they're shopping for hotels. Is the hotel well managed, is it safe, clean, and comfortable? How is the balance between location, service, and price? Politicians and hotel managers have another thing in common: both hotels and countries need paying guests. They'll try to convince you their hotel is the best. For CIs, there's no shortage of choice.

Every country where you're a foreign investor knows that your capital can depart instantly for greener pastures. Like innkeepers, they compete actively for your buck. As a CI, you can leave them if they make it unpleasant or unprofitable to operate within their borders.

12.3 Ways of Obtaining a Second Passport

Birth is the most common way of obtaining citizenship. This is citizenship determined by blood (*jus sanguinis*) or place of birth (jus soli).[92] As a result, you normally obtain the citizenship of your parents. Certain countries even offer passports to descendants further down the line—many Argentinians have Italian or Spanish passports because they descended from immigrants from Italy or Spain. Similar options are open to Irish Americans. I have a friend who received Canadian citizenship through his grandfather who liberated Europe as a soldier of a Native American regiment in the Canadian army. Moreover, he now (temporarily) lives (and works tax free) on an Indian reserve in Canada.

Any child born on its soil can apply for Brazilian citizenship, even if both parents are foreign aliens. The same goes for Americans, which causes a problem with pregnant Chinese citizens flying to the US to give birth.[93] Anchor babies, they're called.

Family ties offer other ways to citizenship; it's standard practice for a spouse to obtain residence, and eventually a citizenship when moving to the country of their spouse. Although it's worth mentioning that in Islamic countries, citizenship can only be passed on through the male line.

Another way of achieving citizenship is the process of "naturalization." A typical way to naturalization is when you have been a resident in a place for an amount of time, typically five years. There can be other qualifications which must be met, such as: being of a certain age, knowing the language, the constitution or the national anthem, having a clean police record, being able to support oneself financially, being in good health, or relinquishing former nationality.[94]

In every country normal procedures can be bypassed. Those useful to a country or its leaders can circumvent normal channels involving citizenship applications, oaths of allegiance, and the usual requirement of several years' residence. Citizenship and passports can be granted immediately and confidentially in any country without notice to anyone.

12.4 Instant Nationality: Citizenship by Investment

Certain countries offer "instantaneous" naturalization (with a couple of months to process) when you invest a substantial sum in the economy. This is called economic citizenship, and only a few countries offer it (although the number is slowly increasing). These programs vary from "cash-for-citizenship" to investing in private sector businesses or property, public works programs, or government debt.

The concept of automatic citizenship is under the microscope. The OECD is now scrutinizing these programs, allegedly because a Russian (you see the pattern?) used a Maltese passport to launder money in Latvia.[95] In addition, it's argued that these kinds of passports can be used to circumvent the CRS. This is funny because the CRS reports on residency, not citizenship. And tax paying is based on residency as well, and you can buy assets in Europe with any passport.

It highlights the contradicting goals of various authorities. On the one hand, we're told we need immigrants to support economies with an aging population. And governments actively target wealthy foreign investors who could have a positive impact. On the other hand, other departments start a witch-hunt for them to protect the "integrity of the financial system."

In any case, passports picked up by investment might, in the future, be more scrutinized when traveling and accessing the financial system. They can be life-savers, but the best way to obtain citizenship remains the "normal" way.

12.5 The Citizenship Selection Process

I spoke to a US client fed up with US politics and citizenship taxation. He was seriously considering renouncing his US citizenship. He married a Filipina, and had attained citizenship in the Philippines. I cautioned him: Filipino citizenship is terrible from a traveling perspective. Filipinos need an exit permit to leave their own country (for their protection, of course). Likewise, the Philippines offers interesting tax benefits with their territorial tax system, but it only applies to foreign nationals, not to Filipino citizens themselves. Moreover, the US has become more hostile to those giving up citizenship by introducing exit-taxes and travel restrictions. He changed his mind.

A number of times, I have been asked by CIs where to move. As if I know what they want? Some need to live in a certain time-zone for work and others can't stand heat (or cold). My first client told me he only wanted to kite-surf. Another didn't like Muslims. Others just care about taxes.

The benefits of having a second passport might be enticing, but don't jump from the frying pan into the fire. Even when you hate your current government, others can be far worse. When picking up a second passport, be sure it makes your life easier, not harder. It has to be from a country unconcerned about what you do outside its borders. You also don't want to receive a letter explaining that you've been drafted into the army. The passport should offer visa-free travel options, not require exit stamps, and ideally be valid for a full ten years. Upon expiration, it should be easily renewable at a consulate or embassy. Do plenty of research. Spend time there. Don't fall for romanticized images.

Check the sentiment. As a minority race, it can be dangerous to be hard working and prosperous. In the large part of the world, wealthy foreigners (or those perceived as such) are specifically targeted by criminals. Think about South Africa, where every other week a family is tortured to death for the crime of putting food on the table.

Other considerations: economic opportunities, cost of living, financial privacy, religious tolerance, social values, stability of government, medical standards, education for your children, the state of the environment, respect for property rights, and personal safety. Ideally you look like the locals, or at least that you don't raise suspicion when walking around with a passport. Make sure to speak the language to avoid unpleasantness at the border. Ideally, select a country with a positive reputation and one which is unlikely to get into disputes with your home country or playgrounds.

12.6 The Power of Diplomatic and Unusual Passports

Diplomatic passports hold mystical power in the eyes of proponents of flag theory. Why? Diplomats make use of the oldest forms of international law:[96] free passage to negotiate with another State and staying on foreign turf without being harmed (even in times of war).

Over the years, these rights have been formalized. They're now codified in the Vienna Convention on Diplomatic Relations (VCDR), Vienna Convention on Consular Relations (VCCR), and the 1969 UN Convention on Special Missions. Diplomats can enjoy two types of immunity.[97] The first, *ratione personae*, enjoys personal immunity by virtue of their office. This is reserved for high level officials only, such as secretaries and ambassadors. The second type, *ratione materiae*, only applies to actions while in office. Even though this is sometimes assumed, the average diplomat can't do whatever he wants. An honorary diplomatic appointment, and the passport going with it, don't conflict with an existing nationality.

The reason diplomatic passports sparked the interest of Flag Theorist was the exemption from administrative burdens, such as not being searched or having to pay income taxes, social security, or customs duties.[98] According to legend, an early "how to" book on how to win such a position sold for 10.000 USD a piece. To my understanding, the quickest way to secure such positions is in African nations, where it's relatively easy to associate with the upper layers of society, make meaningful investments and lobby for their interests.

But let's not forget a fundamental principle of Flag Theory: blend in and mind your own business. The preferential treatment a diplomat enjoys might sound enticing, but it raises suspicion as to what you're doing in their country, especially if you're like me: relatively young, physically fit, and with a military haircut. You might receive a label at odds with reality. From a boring programmer or crypto-trader, you're suddenly a potential threat. Background checks are detailed. You're singled out for questioning. And for what? For not paying taxes you didn't need to pay anyway? To prevent searches that never happen, or to stand in a "special" line at customs with a direct link to the intelligence services?

Diplomatic passports are not a low profile document nor are they good for banking. These days, employees of governments, including diplomats, are designated as Politically Exposed Persons (PEPs), and subjected to Enhanced Due Diligence (EDD). This is to make sure you're not embezzling bribes, or doing other shady stuff. Banks might terminate existing relations rather than dealing with such a "high risk" individual. And close monitoring obligations not only apply to you, but they also apply to your family and close associates (friends and business partners).[99] I'm sure they'll be grateful...

12.6.1 The Ultimate Insider's Club

Nonsurprisingly, Flag Theorists aren't the only figures eying diplomatic benefits. Internationally recognized organizations such as the UN, WHO, IMF, World Bank, Interpol, and who knows how many more, make this their first order of business.

They offer their employees what are called laissez-passers. These travel documents are separate from nationality, but allow the owners to travel, sometimes with diplomatic privileges.[100] Besides travel privileges—COVID restrictions didn't apply to diplomats—these types of organizations free themselves of the national government's influence to ensure their independence. In short: they don't pay taxes. They reveal themselves as hypocrites when their core-mission is to enforce regulations on the rest of us to ensure everybody pays their "fair share" such as with those working for the OECD.[101]

Renowned charities such as the International Red Cross, Doctors without Borders, the Muslim Red Crescent, and the Knights of Malta offer similar travel documents. Perhaps your generous deeds can be rewarded in a tax friendly way!

12.7　Black Passports

Restricted by hefty investments or the time it takes to obtain a passport the natural way, passport hunters resort to the black market. These are offered with the help of corrupt employees, or no real officials at all. Governments do have the power to issue passports, but dubious passports can be retracted by the next group in power. It's simply an unreliable document, which might not even be renewable if something fishy happened with the application. Scams are common also.

In my opinion, fake identity documents are pursued out of stupidity or romantic longings for adventure. There are enough opportunities for adventure: virgin mountains in the Andes and 1000s of medicinal plants to be discovered in jungles around the world. Did you know that Thailand has unexplored caves that poison you if the wind changes?

A common gray area is for a government official to stamp, for a fee of course, a few old stamps in the passport. This "proves" that the minimum amount of time to stay in the country has passed. This might work, but it's not infallible.

Look, identity crime is treated seriously around the world. You don't want to get stuck somewhere in no-man's land with a bogus passport. The more short-cuts you make, the more risk you take. And there is no consumer protection when bribing officials. What are you going to do, call the police? Getting involved with fake passports is not smart. Get a second passport the official way.

13. <Cybersecurity – 7th Flag_

For the average CI, the internet is of paramount importance. Even though the internet made this lifestyle and the existence of cryptos possible, it has downsides. I am not going to comment on securing your wallets or keys. Others are much better with this. What we'll focus on now is privacy.

A war is going on for our privacy (and we're losing). Whether it's the data-mining going on in your social media accounts or the tracking of your phone and financial details. Algorithms are combing through your data, profiling you, mapping what you do, and who you hang out with. Market research, risk profiling, chain analyses, government surveillance, and god knows what else are realities nowadays. If you're not careful, you risk anything you do on the internet being saved forever, scrutinized, analyzed and sold to the highest bidder.

Before we look at how, know that from a legal perspective, cyberspace is subjected to "hyper territorial" behavior of States. They claim jurisdiction based on the smallest of links, including servers' locations, the residence of a client, or the use of a domain extension.[102] For example, all websites with a .com or .org fall under the jurisdiction of the US. And if the website isn't, than at least the data collected by all the US giants such as Google, Facebook, and Microsoft is.

The conscious CI acknowledges that this information can be used against him whenever an algorithm labels him a "risk." Luckily, just as there are States friendly to tax-payers, there are those friendly to data. Flag Theory can be applied in the way you use the internet. Using offshore VPNs, email providers, and hosting servers can reduce the possibility of your data being compromised by nosy individuals, competitors, and governments.

I did not find authoritative sources, but Iceland and Switzerland keep coming up whenever I research this topic. Asian and Arab countries are economically free, but restrict what websites you're allowed to see, blocking controversial topics, but also sites such as Reddit. My advice: don't let others determine what you can see or keep you from your daily dose of memes.

13.1   Virtual Private Network (VPN)

A VPN is the first essential tool. A VPN creates what can be seen as an impenetrable encrypted tunnel through which your data passes without being identified or tracked. This is essential when using Wi-Fi connections at hotels, co-working spaces, and airports. Moreover, it hides your IP address and location, exchanging it with a generic IP address in a country which doesn't police the internet.

Some VPNs let you choose from IP addresses in multiple countries, which can be handy to stream local online television. It's best to use a VPN where your traffic travels through multiple nodes before exiting the tunnel. And your data should not be logged by the network.

13.2   Sheltered Email Service

Email services such as Gmail, Yahoo, and Hotmail work well and are free. But using them without second thought comes at a price. These companies mine and sell your data, and nose around in private conversations.

As a CI, you might want to get a paid email service. They keep your data secure, they do no not mine your contact list, and they don't read your emails. Switzerland is a place where such services are available. Also, try to encrypt your email communication.

13.3   Secure Data Storage

It's easy to use the free cloud storage of companies such as Google. But since the same information applies as with email, you want to volunteer as little sensitive data to them as possible. You can store previously encrypted files or look for a secure alternative.

The foremost protection method for files in the cloud is encryption. If you know what you're doing, with proper encryption, you can even use free services. Even better are fully encrypted cloud services. These sites are so secure, that without your password, no one can access what's stored. You're responsible, and if you lose your password, that's it; you lost access to your data.

13.4   Password Mastery

All the passwords CIs must use are impossible to remember. Some still use excel or word files to save them, or use variations of the same basic password. This is a major security risk. Password manager apps offer a solution. They allow for large, complex passwords to be stored and easily copied into websites. They are encrypted with one master password. IF this password is strong, they are practically impossible to crack. However, this password should be remembered well and be kept safe, as it allows access to everything.

13.5   Configure Your Computer for Privacy

If you're serious about privacy, hiding your IP and encrypting your data is not enough. Tracking also happens through your own computer. Your browser for example, is a treasure trove of information. To prevent this, use open source browsers such as Firefox, delete cookies and browsing history upon closing, don't save passwords, and turn off geolocation. Next, you can install plug-ins to block ads, malicious scripts, and "local shared objects" (supercookies).[103] One thing you'll notice is that privacy enhancing measures reduce how easy the browser works. Ultimately, you determine how far you take it.

If you use Windows, the auto-settings include data-mining. Think about using Linux instead (which is also less vulnerable to viruses). The same applies to your Smartphone. Check app permissions and if they seem invasive or unnecessary, pass the app in favor of another.

On a final note, don't fool yourself that with these measures alone free you from snooping eyes. There are probably hundreds of other ways for tracking your activity, especially with targeted surveillance. The combination of your browser, add-ons, time-zone, and operating system already creates a "finger print" you leave everywhere you go.

As with Flag Theory in general, it's a process. You want to start with basic measures to prevent your data floating around the internet. Regain more and more in control. You might have to educate your girlfriend or wife on this as well, since women tend to share everything without second thought.

13.6   Secure Web-Hosting

Be mindful where you host your websites. There have been cases where the location of the servers create a permanent establishment and a tax liability.[104] Moreover, huge differences exist between countries as to how they protect your identity and data. Have your website hosted in a place where they respect privacy, where they don't bother with what you publish, and where you can securely store your data (especially when writing about sensitive topics).

13.7   Planned Data Distribution

Remember what I wrote about banking: there is no hiding from the data-monsters, especially for a CI. In fact, it might be suspicious if nothing can be found about you. Try to control what ends up in common databases and what you post to promote yourself. At the same time, conceal sensitive matters.

Also, try to think about how companies perceive you. Logging in with an unknown IP address, can result in you ending up in a foreign land without access to your bank account. Keeping data in these databases is essential, but at least manage what is being mined.

Don't volunteer data. Don't fill in surveys to discover which Game of Thrones character you are, don't allow apps to mine your data, and don't volunteer sensitive information in forums. Don't fill in unnecessary surveys. Don't trust regulations to ensure your privacy. And don't trust governments and large organizations to keep your data secure—*they won't*...

14.   <Final Steps of Prudence_

In the previous chapters we looked at the tax aspects of international living and the Flags recommended for increasing your liberty. Having had many talks with international entrepreneurs over the years, various misunderstood topics keep coming back. I combined them in this chapter.

14.1 Health Insurance

As discussed, by venturing out of your (mandatory) national systems, you discover what a free market is. Nowhere is this more obvious than in healthcare. Those living in the Western world have, over the decades, come to believe that healthcare is a right and not an (expensive) commodity requiring advanced equipment, highly educated doctors, nurses, and prime real estate. You'll be cured quickly of this illusion when you get sick on holiday and the doctor politely asks you to pay in advance. Haggling, price shopping, scamming, it all happens. There are doctors making extra cash by selling you things you don't need, from a relativity innocent overpriced bandage to unnecessary surgery.

Turkish hospitals came under scrutiny when they took out their patient's appendix at the first sign of cramp or food poisoning. The naive Dutchies believed it all since "the private clinic looked so nice!" and the health insurance paid anyway. One summer holiday, I took an injured friend to the emergency room. He said he was beaten up, but had no visible damage. The doctors made a big fuss, told us the damage was permanent, did all sorts of tests and shoved tubes up his nose and penis. In the end he had nothing but a big hospital bill. This was not in a third world country but in Spain!

In Bali, I visited a German "doctor" who did a life blood analysis and told me I had parasites in my liver since the red blood-cells clotted together. She prescribed me an herbal medicine. After I did research back home I learned she had showed me blood cells which had naturally dried up outside the body. All the positive reviews of "Doctor Peggy" (she wasn't a doctor), meant many went along with it. When in Cambodia, I read about a French doctor who prescribed nose-spray for everything, even life-threatening illnesses. The only reliable healthcare service in this country seemed to be a flight to either Singapore or Thailand.

Having said all this, in the few countries with a (relatively) free market in healthcare system such as Thailand or Singapore, the hospitals compete on quality, price, and service. You can get better care at a better price in a top hospital in Thailand than in your hometown. I was told by an American who supplied hospitals for a living that the famous Bumrungrad hospital in Bangkok was better equipped than any hospital he knew in the US.

If you're young and healthy, you might end up with lower insurance costs compared to your national plan. Buy one insurance and stick with it. I see people hopping and price shopping, using local plans for a few years, or plans offered by employers. But insurance is to prevent bankruptcy in case you can't pay. If you fall seriously ill, and a big bill comes at the end of your contract, good luck claiming it or finding a new policy. Remember, nobody needs to do business with you in a free market, and if you're already sick nobody will! Get a product for life, big daddy government isn't here to hold your hand.

14.2 Don't Break the Law!

Not everybody understands the current regulatory environment. This one guy emailed me for a "secure" bank account (as in a bank account where nobody can find out who's behind it). I told him this no longer exists. He returned a slightly impatient email, again explaining what he needed, and asking if I otherwise knew somebody who knew his trade. I hate to pop anyone's bubble, but a truly confidential bank account no longer exists, nor is it necessary for a CI to pursue. There are ways to reduce taxes while observing the law and keeping peace of mind.

Evading taxes creates "black money;" money you cannot easily use or wire to your personal bank account without potential alarm bells going off. This might start out easily, by setting up a semi-anonymous structure where you take out spending money with an ATM card. If your business grows, you suddenly realize these small amounts via the ATM don't cut it. Now it starts to live a life of its own. One day, the rules change, and your bank labels you a risk and cancels the relationship. You now have four weeks to look for a place where your funds can be wired. And it has to be in your personal name. This is the moment when you start to lose control and risk far more than you might have gained in tax savings. If you really have been a naughty boy, you might start receiving letters from the tax office. Now you're in full-on crisis mode. This is not freedom.

It's worse when you don't have a clue what you're doing. I had a client who was supposed to move to Dubai (I repeat = no income taxes). I set up a costly structure for him, requiring ample paperwork and months to complete. When the company was finally set up, I asked when he was going to apply for the visa to move over. He asked me what I was thinking. He wasn't going to move to "that desert." He was going to "register" himself with a friend (not how it works in Dubai), and "subscribe to Donald Duck" to prove he was living there. In reality, he stayed back in Europe and expected to not have to pay taxes. He added that I had said this was possible.

First comment. The "some guy told me this was possible" argument is not enough when YOU end up in a dispute (unless you have a written tax opinion). Secondly, if you're financially illiterate better keep things simple. I met many people who solely relied on advisers. But the same laws apply to all. Make sure to understand what you're getting yourself into. Depending on others is the exact opposite of freedom.

Also, current developments go rapidly towards openness and transparency. The chances of getting caught increase significantly every year. Ten years ago, you could walk into a Swiss bank with a suitcase filled with cash. Nowadays, they just as easily kick an honest client out after forty years if you live in certain European countries or the US of A.

Every now and then I get emails from people hell-bent on changing reality in their favor. They have something in mind, and only want me to confirm it. I cannot convince them, not even when referring to the law. When they don't like what I say, they go to someone who tells them what they want to hear. The "how they got away with it" stories are cute and might impress cheap women. Given the interconnectedness of the system and databases such as World-Check, missteps can have lasting consequences. Avoid taking unnecessary risks. Don't cross the line between exploiting legal loopholes and blatant illegality.

Keep a low profile, and stay out of trouble with the law. Avoid confrontations with anyone. Don't trust anyone in "authority." Don't uncritically accept all the stuff in this book as gospel truth either! It might be outdated or not applicable to you... View "experts" with suspicion. Be tolerant of other opinions. Use common sense. Above all, *never* be tied to one system.

14.3 Things that Suck About Being an Expat

Here are aspects of the expat life not advertised. Expats often enjoy life and ignore the local politics and what happens around them. They can be so blinded by the good, they ignore the (really) bad.

First of all, as an expat, you're still dealing with bureaucracy. Perhaps even more so! Especially the tight balance of dealing with visas can be a pain. It means driving to immigration offices on the other side of town, wasting time, and undergoing privacy sensitive mundane and meaningless procedures. Entire departments of traffic police in various countries in Asia target tourists for fines / bribes.

Both my old employer and I had no problem advocating for the economic liberty we found in Dubai. But one day, I browsed a local news site with the summaries of four articles: a father who whipped his son to death for having bad marks; a Brazilian guy who tried to flee after killing a pedestrian while speeding and under the influence of alcohol; an Angolan kid (with connections) who lost control while drunk and speeding and drove his SUV into a restaurant, killing three diners; and finally, a drunk UK party animal who was running through the apartment building in his underwear, causing a scene. Question: who spent the most time in jail? ... The two drivers were released after a few months and kicked out of the country (maybe bribes?). The father was released after a few months thanks to fact that the grandparents were unwilling to pursue charges against their own child. The Briton? He spent seven months in jail. The word "justice" doesn't come to mind.

One of the things you experience as a CI is that your access to financial systems starts to match those from the developing world. It becomes a balancing act. Every international payment might trigger a freeze of your account. Every moment your bank might ask you for due diligence documents you don't have. If you lose your ATM card, they send a replacement to your registered address—*where you lived three years ago*. Installing a bank app on a phone with the wrong telephone number? They might freeze the account to see what's going on.

Traveling itself is not comfortable or glamorous. You can get sick of it after a while, especially when it's forced upon you by previously mentioned visa issues. It's difficult to focus on work or truly build a business if your entire life is uprooted every two months when you have to move. In practice, it can be difficult to sell your services from the other side of the world. And let's not forget the Wi-Fi or electricity which stops working when you're talking to a client.

These downsides don't measure up against the upsides. But it's not always fun and easy.

14.4   Don't Air Your Fiscal Laundry

You leave a large group of family and friends behind after moving abroad. And even though you're on the other side of the world, you can easily keep in contact and will likely return home often. Even when you love the principles of this book, and delight in your newborn freedom, refrain from informing anyone about it.

The group of people looking for ultimate freedom is small. Challenging the system, and making deliberate attempts to "get out" upsets folks—*especially those whose salary depends on tax payers*. The general populous ties its entire identity to a certain system, and those not taking part become outcasts. You have given up on your patriotic duty. You chickened out. Don't think you're not the target of envy. They might hate or secretly undermine you. Or at least bring it up a little bit too often...

The same is true for those you run into on the road, whether locals, holidaymakers, or expats. They likely pay taxes and can't stand those paying less. Expect all sorts of mental gymnastics. At a dinner, I had someone claiming the moral high-ground by stating he recently paid all his taxes in the UK. Funnily, he lived and worked without a permit in Indonesia, breaking both tax and immigration laws. And one call to Her Majesty's Revenue and Customs would've informed him he is not obliged to pay them anything. [105]

Even if you do things legally, it's still best not to advertise what you're doing. If you flaunt your activities or openly mock authorities it could influence a decision against you. And when a loophole is publicized enough, the government may try to close it. And remember: what is legal might not be how people think it should be.

14.5 When in a Dispute with the (Tax) Authorities

Though uncommon, it might be possible to end up in the cross-hairs of the authorities. Don't be intimidated. Governments often intimidate people to scare them into handing over information "voluntarily." When you receive a letter, they might not have anything. There might be a misunderstanding or they're fishing. It doesn't refrain them from making all sorts of assumptions about the situation though, attempting to trick you. Answering incorrectly might get you into trouble, though.

First of all, be friendly and cooperative. You're a number to them. It's not personal. Stay calm and don't get emotional. Being disassociated from the outcome is the surviving mechanism of those working in the legal system.

Don't be a pompous twat. Government employees are (somewhat) human as well. They can be motivated by envy, especially if you're living the life of your dreams, and they're living in quiet desperation.

The best way of winning a dispute is by not being in one. This sounds logical, but an awful lot of people start traveling without making proper arrangements. They make a mess, bumping through life as if in a pinball machine. Making tax planning work is less effort than running from one half-baked solution to the next. Take time to think this through. Understand the laws. The rebel is the other side of the same coin. Don't fight the current; swim with it.

Make sure you document everything. Especially during a process of immigration. It's surprising how blurred your memory becomes after a few years of pub crawls. Especially with respect to crucial information for tax authorities such as dates, periods you stayed where, or when you corresponded with which official. Create a record of the process and all your evidence. Always communicate by letter or email in order to track what happened. An employee can be helpful on the phone in explaining matters but in a dispute the "someone told me this by telephone" argument is worth nothing.

Reverse their tactics. If they include term limits (answer this letter in two weeks), set your own. Give *them* two weeks to respond. It establishes yourself as a serious person. Don't accept unreasonable treatment. It will not save you, but it might help in the question of guilt and determining the severity of a possible sentence. You wouldn't be the first organized and reasonable tax payer who sees his case dismissed by a judge due to fishing by an unorganized and unreasonable tax authority.

15. <Americans (and Green Card Holders)_

Unfortunately, ultimate tax freedom is not available to US citizens. They are taxed based on citizenship, not on residency. In the following section, I summarize the reporting and tax obligations for Americans and Green Card holders. Keep in mind that this is an area in development. While the overall principles will likely remain the same, the details might be obsolete the moment you read this. Always make sure you base your decisions on up-to-date information, or get professional advice.

15.1 Filing Tax Returns

As a US citizen, you're almost always required to file a US tax return, unless you make less than 12.000 USD in gross income as a single person under 65. Gross income is all income you receive in the form of money, goods, property, and services that is not exempt from tax. If your net earnings from self-employment are $400 or more, you must file a return even if your gross income is below the amount listed above. In short, there appears little to be done as an entrepreneurial CI to prevent you from having to file for taxes, unless you decide to live somewhere for under $1.000 a month. These are 2018 numbers.[106]

In the instructions on form 1040 for 2019, it clearly states that: "if, in 2019, you engaged in a transaction involving virtual currency you will need to file Schedule 1."[107] On Schedule 1, you can see the infamous check-box, asking if:

"at any time during 2019, did you receive, sell, send, exchange, or otherwise acquire any financial interest in any virtual currency?"[108]

Virtual currencies are treated as property for federal tax purposes.[109] As stated in Notice 2014-21: "In general, the sale or exchange of convertible virtual currency, or the use of convertible virtual currency to pay for goods or services in a real-world economy transaction, has tax consequences that may result in a tax liability."[110] The sale of crypto-currencies for real or other virtual currencies can result in a capital gain (or loss).[111] There is a distinction in assets held longer, and shorter than one year, and capital gains are calculated using Form 8948.[112] Capital gains and losses are reported in Schedule D (attached to form 1040).[113]

15.2   Reporting of Accounts

Besides tax returns, there is the reporting of foreign accounts to the Treasury Department. Each United States person, including a citizen, resident, corporation, partnership, limited liability company, trust and estate, must file a FBAR to report:

- a financial interest in or signature or other authority over at least one financial account located outside the United States if
- the aggregate value of those foreign financial accounts exceeded $10,000 at any time during the calendar year reported.[114]

Another "thingy" is FATCA, implemented to discourage US tax payers[115] from hiding financial assets from the IRS in foreign bank accounts. Under FATCA, a single US tax payer living abroad must file Form 8938 if the total value of their foreign financial assets is more than $200.000 on the last day of the tax year, or more than $300.000 at any time during the year.[116] Not reporting on a foreign account could bring a fine of 10.000 USD per year. In addition, unpaid taxes will be collected—*plus an additional 40 percent as penalty*.[117]

As of now, there is no clear guidance if virtual currency held in a foreign exchange is reportable. The main reason is that virtual currencies are considered property. Normally, foreign accounts are denominate in currency.

In terms of FBAR, regulatory body FinCEN responded that the regulations do not define virtual currency held in an offshore account as a type of reportable account.[118] In terms of FATCA, I could not find any official guidance. My guess is that the trend of more transparency continues. Moreover, the exchanges might already report your data to the IRS. Play it safe.

Having said that, as a US Citizen, you still can benefit from Flag Theory, tax planning, and moving to a country with fewer rules. There are, to my knowledge, four forms of legal tax planning. These have been around for a while so they will likely exist in the future.

15.3   Tax Free Salary

As an American resident of a foreign country, you can earn a certain amount of income that is tax exempt by the IRS. This is, at the time of writing, 103.900 USD per year,[119] an amount you can live a comfortable life with in most countries in the world.

To claim the foreign earned income exclusion, the foreign housing exclusion, or the foreign housing deduction (more on that below), you must meet all three of the following requirements:

1) Your tax home must be in a foreign country.
2) You must have foreign earned income.
3) You must be one of the following.
    a. A US. citizen who is a bona fide resident of a foreign country or countries for an uninterrupted period that includes an entire tax year.
    b. A US. resident alien who is a citizen or national of a country with which the United States has an income tax treaty in effect and who is a bona fide resident of a foreign country or countries for an uninterrupted period that includes an entire tax year.
    c. A US. citizen or a resident alien who is physically present in a foreign country or countries for at least 330 full days during any period of 12 consecutive months.[120]

Eligible for the exclusion is pay for personal services performed, such as: salaries and wages, commissions, bonuses, professional fees, and tips.[121] Even the income earned by self-employed people working through a sole proprietorship or partnership can be eligible as long as capital is not an income-producing factor.[122] Providing personal services (working) is leading here. Even if you own your own corporation, it can pay you for personal services. As long as this allowance is reasonable.[123]

As a reminder, various kinds of income each attract distinct taxes. This exclusion is specifically for income tax. It doesn't apply to the reporting intensive tax on capital gains discussed earlier. However, if you get paid a salary in Bitcon, for example for working for an exchange, this could work. And I can promise you that with 103.900 USD you can live like a king almost anywhere in the world.

15.4   Tax Free Home

In addition to the foreign earned income exclusion, you can claim an exclusion or a deduction from gross income for your housing costs if your tax home is in a foreign country. You must qualify for the exclusions and deductions under either the bona fide residence test or the physical presence test.

The housing *exclusion* applies only to amounts considered paid for with employer-provided amounts. The housing *deduction* applies only to amounts paid for with self-employment earnings. The maximum amount deductible is $16,624, or $45.55 per day.[124]

15.5   Foreign Tax Credit

The foreign tax credit reduces the double tax burden that would otherwise arise when foreign source income is taxed by both the United States and the foreign country from which the income is derived.[125] This is not a method to not pay taxes, but it at least ensures you don't pay taxes twice. And other than only applying to personal services as the previous two examples, the foreign tax credit applies to any type of income, for example dividends or capital gains.

The Foreign Tax Credit is a product of US tax law, so no need to apply a tax treaty. In short, if you paid taxes on a certain income abroad, a US tax payer can generally deduct this from what he pays from the tax bill back home.

15.6   Use of Corporations

For US citizens living outside of the US, an offshore corporate structure *might* defer tax payments. How does this work? Within a company structure, the operating company pays out its profit to the parent company. This parent company, instead of paying the shareholder a profit, uses the funds to increase business activities, pay for business expenses, or buy assets (such as a house, boat, or investment portfolio). Also, this new business can benefit from a low regulatory environment and cheaper labor.

One other benefit of using a corporate structure is setting up a trading company. If you can set up a company that trades crypto-currencies on your behalf, you might be able to avoid complicated capital gains reporting and tax obligations. You would then be paid a monthly salary (of course matching out the foreign income exclusion above), and pay yourself an annual dividend. Keep in mind that corporations bring other reporting obligations. And typical offshore jurisdictions have (sometimes strict) regulations for cryptos as well.

This is not a do it yourself area, due to possible tax and reporting complications and specific rules for passive investments and offshore companies. This is just a general idea.

<Afterword: The Road to True Liberty_

Thank you for reading this book! I trust it has given you great new perspectives! Knowledge is power. Maybe there are certain areas where you now can say: no thanks. You can take steps to arrange your economic affairs as you see fit. The same laws that force you to comply, also spell out when you don't have to.

If you adopt the advice in this book, you operate from a position of strength and sovereignty. This is a great feeling. You play by the rules, but you decide when to bet or fold. From just a pawn on the board, you become the king. It is special to be able to live this way. The artist of your own life. Paint it with a wonderful brush!

But with great power, comes responsibility. And now that I have provided you with tools to improve your life, I have to make one more point.

I did not plan to write this book. My goal is to be a pioneering part of the decentralized revolution. One of the opportunities we have in crypto is to rethink how society functions. Central banks and governments have demonstrated that they cannot be trusted with the money supply. And yes, this power needs to be taken away from them. But it isn't the only thing that we need to do, and it is no longer the most important.

We are controlled through laws. And even though many nowadays understand how money is created out of thin air, few understand how laws are increasingly created in a similarly perverted fashion. Legal systems are just as misused, and in a far more invasive manner than the monetary system. Moreover, this process is quickly getting out of control.

Do you remember when I explained how the Panama Papers resulted in tight regulation and monitoring of the financial system? This process is now expanding to all walks of life. The way it works is as follows: take an existing problem, magnify it through the media, claim the problem is "to big for countries to handle on their own," and then offer a solution by shifting more power to (new) unaccountable supranational organizations.

Next, you create guidance and protocols and have them signed by members of national governments. These laws now supersede the national laws (and democratic oversight). Politicians eagerly sign away all the rights entrusted to them by their citizens. They know that if they play the game, they end up in privileged positions with immunity without taxes or having to answer to something—err someone—as primitive as voters. Look at the increasing force of organizations such as the OECD, the UN, and the EU. A corrupt parasite from Ethiopia at the WHO said "this is a pandemic" and protocols are set in motion keeping everyone indoors while 100s of millions of tax payer dollars flow to big pharma.[126] That is power.

The reason all exchanges have the same KYC, is the same reason all governments attack the same liberties during COVID-19. Without going into too much detail, the tool used is international law. This is a type of law created by countries when they sign a treaty. If you look at most constitutions, you will see that there is a clause stating that international treaties supersede national law. And this is the back-door. Politicians increasingly sign, often under pressure, large agreements with multinational organizations on energy, environment, health, education, finance, and food production. Every treaty siphons off more power to international bureaucrats. The average voter has no say in this.

I see an awakening of people who feel something is wrong. Not knowing what it is, they often resort to conspiracy theories. But it happens in the open and you realize it once you are able to look past the nonsense in the media and the acting of national politicians pretending to still decide things.

I understand that it might be overwhelming that a lot of what you assume is your political process is actually a charade. A play to sell you on something already decided. But there you have it. And moreover, there is nothing you can do about it and it is now starting to affect your ability to travel, what you can and cannot say on social media, and soon what blockchain you can use. Unless we stop it, it will expand.

My goal is to not only shed light on this process, but also offer an alternative. Decentralized money has proven so primordially attractive that there is nothing stopping it. But we think too small... The process of decentralization can, and should be expanded. And once your hodlings have gone to the moon, and you're living a sovereign life, you can think: what's next?

In big lines, we have to do the following:

Step 1. Decentralized money. Of course, many brilliant minds are already working on this. From what I am seeing, a truly decentralized payment system is underway. That still doesn't mean we are out of the woods. We need stronger privacy systems, more peer-to-peer interaction and actual payments, and a silent resistance to all issues of centralization.

Step 2. Reestablish our rights. We need a sort of global Magna Carta. If there is one thing I learned from studying the rule of law and liberty, is that they should be seen as limitations on the powerful, rather than the rights of the powerless. Governments don't ensure human rights, human right laws are supposed to protect us from them. Governments keep chipping away at liberties until they are stopped. It needs to be made clear to them in a unified effort what they are and aren't allowed to do.

Step 3. National efforts. We must elect politicians who understand the international power grab. As much as crypto enthusiasts bitch about their government, at least they are (somewhat) accountable. Right now, they are the quickest way to end this process. All that is needed to is to resign from international treaties that are not in the nation's best interest. It is very simple, and yet the consequences are real. It is similar to not repaying a loan; if you default, nobody wants to loan you money anymore. The moment you start resigning from international treaties, the entire international community declares you an enemy of the social order (examples are Brexit, Donald Trump, Sweden and Belarus during corona). It takes balls to chip away at the roots of international power structures and instead look after the national and individual interest. But now is the time to do so.

Step 4. Decentralized Law. Next, we must govern our own interactions. Those currently in power don't understand anything about this space and how it shapes the future. They should not be relied upon, or allowed to regulate any innovation out of existence. We can be more proactive in writing our own laws to govern this space. Why wait for the government to write theirs? Be proactive. We can create our own jurisdiction by consent, before it is enforced.

There is nothing stopping a large collection of private individuals from writing their own laws. This is already done by private international sports organizations, such as the FIFA and the IOC, who have their own court system with force in the real world. The same can be created for the decentralized space.

To facilitate this, I have created a framework for Decentralized Law. It is based on open source software and is similar to open source development processes used for Bitcoin. Moreover, it complements existing working legal systems. Even better, it is surprisingly easy to create.

Join me in this quest of decentralizing more than just money alone. I have seen liberty erode at a rapid pace over the last couple of years, and there might be a moment when you can no longer hideout in any corner of the world.

Join me now, for a free and just world...

Go here to Learn More:
www.decentralizedlegalsystem.com

Follow me on Twitter!
@Decentral_Law

<Notes_

---

[1] Thysse, W., *"The Decentralized Legal System—the First Framework for Decentralized Law,"* (Decentralized Legal System, VERSION 1.2, 27-08-2018), available at: https://decentralizedlegalsystem.com/

[2] *"Social Contract Theory,"* (Internet Encyclopedia of Philosophy), accessed on July 1, 2019, https://www.iep.utm.edu/soc-cont/: *"the view that persons' moral and/or political obligations are dependent upon a contract or agreement among them to form the society in which they live."*

[3] EU, *"Consolidated versions of the Treaty on European Union and the Treaty on the Functioning of the European Union - Consolidated version of the Treaty on the Functioning of the European Union - Protocols - Annexes - Declarations annexed to the Final Act of the Intergovernmental Conference which adopted the Treaty of Lisbon, signed on 13 December 2007,"* https://eur-lex.europa.eu/legal-content/EN/TXT/HTML/?uri=CELEX:12012E/TXT&from=EN : Article 21 *"1. Every citizen of the Union shall have the right to move and reside freely within the territory of the Member States, subject to the limitations and conditions laid down in the Treaties and by the measures adopted to give them effect."*

[4] *"Free movement of persons,"* (Fact Sheets of the European Union), accessed on July 1, 2019, https://europarl.europa.eu/factsheets/en/sheet/147/free-movement-of-persons:
"a. Rights and obligations:

> ** For stays of under three months: the only requirement for Union citizens is that they possess a valid identity document or passport. The host Member State may require the persons concerned to register their presence in the country.*
> ** For stays of over three months: EU citizens and their family members — if not working — must have sufficient resources and sickness insurance to ensure that they do not become a burden on the social services of the host Member State during their stay. Union citizens do not need residence permits, although Member States may require them to register with the authorities. Family members of Union citizens who are not nationals of a Member State must apply for a residence permit, valid for the duration of their stay or a five-year period.*
> ** Right of permanent residence: Union citizens acquire this right after a five-year period of uninterrupted legal residence, provided that an expulsion decision has not been enforced against them. This right is no longer subject to any conditions. The same rule applies to family members who are not nationals of a Member State and who have lived with a Union citizen for five years. The right of permanent residence is lost only in the event of more than two successive years' absence from the host Member State.*
> ** Restrictions on the right of entry and the right of residence: Union citizens or members of their family may be expelled from the host Member State on grounds of public policy, public security or public health. Guarantees are provided to ensure that such decisions are not taken on economic grounds, comply with the proportionality principle and are based on personal conduct, among others."*

[5] *"Taxation,"* (European Union), accessed on 1 July 2019, https://europa.eu/european-union/topics/taxation_en: *"The EU does not have a direct role in collecting taxes or setting tax rates. The amount of tax each citizen pays is decided by their national government, along with how the collected taxes are spent."* [Author: they should have used resident here: because no State in the EU taxes based on citizenship]

[6] Ferris, T., *"The 4-hour workweek: escape 9-5, live anywhere, and join the new rich,"* First Edition (Crown Publishers, New York 2007), page 113

[7] *"A new ICIJ investigation exposes a rogue offshore industry,"* (International Consortium of Investigative Journalists, April 3, 2019), accessed on July 1, 2019, https://www.icij.org/blog/2016/04/new-icij-investigation-exposes-rogue-offshore-industry/

[8] Obermayer, B., *"How two German newspaper reporters broke the story behind the Panama Papers,"* (Quartz, July 12, 2016). Author: the initial research into the Panama Papers (allegedly) unveiled Argentinean, Russian and German officials.

[9] *"Super rich hold $32 trillion in offshore havens,"* (Reuters, Business News, July 22, 2012), accessed on July 3, 2019, https://www.reuters.com/article/us-offshore-wealth/super-rich-hold-32-trillion-in-offshore-havens-idUSBRE86L03U20120722

[10] Henry, James S., *"The Price of Offshore Revisited - New Estimates For Missing Global Private Wealth, Income, Inequality, And Lost Taxes,"* (Tax Justice Network, July 2012), https://taxjustice.net/cms/upload/pdf/Price_of_Offshore_Revisited_120722.pdf: [Author Note] I checked the 32 Trillion USD mentioned in the Reuters article. It comes from a report by the Tax Justice Network, a lobby group trying to convince the world we need to tax more to combat inequality, climate change and other noble causes. They have an ideological and personal (their jobs) incentive to paint a picture of an out of control financial sector. The first support for their estimate of *"$21 trillion to $32 estimate for global offshore financial assets as of 2010"* comes from taking the *"private banking assets under management at the top 50 international private banks for the period 2005-2010"* and assuming large annual increases, underreported assets and other managed assets (p33).

First of all, they assume that everyone banking at an top 50 private bank hides his money offshore. Nonsense. Next, the actual $21 trillion to $32 estimate is based on an *"Offshore Investor Portfolio Profile"* (p34) which scaled *"BIS data on offshore deposits by 'nonbanks'"* introducing a *"liquidity ratio"* based on estimates of asset allocations for high net worth portfolios. In short, they look at how much money rich people have in the bank to guess what else they have and add it to their net-worth. I have four problems with this: firstly, it assumes that the rest of their portfolio is invested offshore. Even if wealthy entrepreneurs might keep financial assets offshore, it doesn't (at all) guarantee that the rest of their assets are. Take for example the house that they live in; it is included in this number but it is hard to hide a American house in the Cayman Islands (I dare say almost impossible). Secondly, it creates a fictional volume of assets sitting in offshore banks outside of the financial system. But this money isn't buried in the sand, it is invested in bank deposits, shares, government bonds and real estate in solid jurisdictions. All these streams of capital are regulated and often taxed at source. Next, it paints a picture that all cross-border activities are dodgy, while I still think it is perfectly normal for someone to own a holiday home in Southern Europe or invest in Africa. Fourth and finally, the report makes a wide estimate, but the Reuters article only focuses on the largest number for shock-effect.

[11] Nestmann, M., *"Government "Stats" Strike Again,"* (Nestmann, March 25, 2014), accessed on July 3, 2019, https://www.nestmann.com/government-stats-strike-again. [Author note] In this article it is explained how the US media, congress, and Barack Obama got into a frenzy over an alleged $150 Billion USD lost tax income due to offshore tax avoidance. The number turned out to have been made up ("guessed") by Jack Blum, an attorney and former congressional researcher.

[12] I saw this comment being made on Reddit and by Andreas Antonopoulos during an interview.

[13] OECD, *"International tax avoidance and evasion: four related studies,"* (OECD, Committee on Fiscal Affairs, Paris, 1987), page 11

[14] Ibid., page 11: Not a direct quote, but a summary of the three elements of tax avoidance as per the OECD report.

[15] Finnerty C.J., Merks P., et al, *"Fundamentals of International Tax Planning,"* (IBFD, July 2007), available at: https://www.ibfd.org/IBFD-Products/Fundamentals-International-Tax-Planning, page 49:
"Less clear is the distinction between 'tax avoidance' and 'tax planning', the latter also known as 'acceptable tax avoidance'. The borderline here is typically rather unclear since the vast majority of countries recognize the right of taxpayers to arrange their affairs in a way that attracts minimum tax liability. On the other hand, behaviors that are solely or mainly tax driven are generally counteracted with legislative or judicial provision."

[16] Idib., These examples ar summarized on page 51 of *Fundamentals of International Tax Planning*. To include actual court cases and context is far beyond the scope of this book. There is nothing wrong with tax planning, ok?

[17] Ibid., pages 66-69 define substantive tax planning and provide images for each variation.

[18] *"Global Compact For Safe, Orderly and Regular Migration (Marrakesh Pact),"* (UN, Global Compact For Migration, July 11, 2018), https://refugeesmigrants.un.org/sites/default/files/180711_final_draft_0.pdf, objective 15: Provide access to basic services for migrants; rights to schooling and health care for migrants are mentioned in point e and f.

[19] Buterin, V., *"A Next-Generation Smart Contract and Decentralized Application Platform,"* (2013) accessed April 4, 2018, https://github.com/ethereum/wiki/wiki/White-Paper

[20] Thysse, W., *"The Decentralized Legal System—the First Framework for Decentralized Law,"* (2018)

[21] Baker, P., *"Binance CEO Changpeng "CZ" Zhao really doesn't want to tell you where his firm's headquarters is located,"* (Coindesk, May 8, 2020), accessed on September 17, 2020, https://www.coindesk.com/binance-doesnt-have-a-headquarters-because-bitcoin-doesnt-says-ceo:

the articles quotes CZ who says: *"Well, I think what this is is the beauty of the blockchain, right, so you don't have to …[author: have a head-office]... like where's the Bitcoin office, because Bitcoin doesn't have an office."*

[22] Thysse W., *"Lesson 5 – What is a Decentralized Consensus Jurisdiction?"* (Decentralized Law Lessons, December 28, 2019), available on:
https://decentralizedlegalsystem.com/law/consensus-jurisdiction/

[23] *"Montevideo Convention on the Rights and Duties of States,"* (Montevideo, 26 December 1933), accessed on June 24, 2019,
https://www.ilsa.org/jessup/jessup15/Montevideo%20Convention.pdf: Article 1

[24] Oppenheim L., Jennings Sir R., and Watts, Sir A. (eds), *"Oppenheim's International Law,"* 9th edition (Harlow: Longman, 1992): p456.
Author: the original definition provided the European Union as an example of a regulatory body, but I removed it since the EU as of now (luckily) does not have taxing rights, and would just confuse readers.

[25] *"INTERNATIONAL BUSINESS COMPANIES ACT, 2016,"* (Supplement of the Official Gazette, Seychelles, 10th August 2016, Act 15 0f 2016):

> *PART II – COMPANY INCORPORATION - Sub-Part I—*
>
> *5.(1) Types of international business companies:*
>
> *An "international business company" means a company incorporated or continued, or converted into a company, under this Act and whose memorandum states that it is subject to the restrictions referred to in subsection (2)*
>
> *5.(2) A company shall* **_not_***— (a) subject to subsection (3),* **carry on business in Seychelles;**
>
> *PART XXI – MISCELLANEOUS PROVISIONS*
>
> *361.(1) A company, including all the income and profits of a company, is* **exempt from the Business Tax Act.**

[26] Finnerty C.J., Merks P., et al, (2007), page 5: made small alteration for readability.

[27] Ibid., page 8: made small alteration for readability.

[28] *"COMMISSIONER OF INTERNAL REVENUE, vs. JULIANE BAIER-NICKEL, G.R. No. 153793,"* August 29, 2006, Philippines Supreme Court, Manila, First Division.

[29] Finnerty C.J., Merks P., et al, (2007), page 5: Almost this entire paragraph comes from the section: 2.1 general. Made small alteration for readability.

[30] Finnerty C.J., Merks P., et al, (2007), page 13: *"A State cannot base the exercise of its tax jurisdiction on the fact that under the relevant tax treaty it may tax a certain item of income. Double tax treaties only limit the exercise of taxing rights, they cannot create new ones."*

[31] Canada-United Kingdom Tax Convention, as signed on September 8, 1978 and

amended by the Protocols signed on April 15, 1980 and October 16, 1985, accessed on July 4, 2019:

https://assets.publishing.service.gov.uk/government/uploads/system/uploads/attac hment_data/file/496655/canada1978-dta2014-consol_-_in_force.pdf,

"Article 10 Dividends:

1. *Dividends paid by a company which is a resident of a Contracting State to a resident of the other Contracting State may be taxed in that other State.*

2. *However, such dividends may also be taxed in the Contracting State of which the company paying the dividends is a resident and according to the laws of that State, but if the beneficial owner of the dividends is a resident of the other Contracting State the tax so charged shall not exceed:*

    a) *5 per cent of the gross amount of the dividends if the beneficial owner is a company which controls, directly or indirectly, at least 10 per cent of the voting power in the company paying the dividends;*

    b) *15 per cent of the gross amount of the dividends in all other cases."*

Based on this one might assume that an individual living in Canada receiving a dividend from the UK is taxed in the UK at 15% before being taxed in Canada on the same income. However, there is no dividend tax at source in the UK. Those just looking at tax treaties are misinformed.

[32] *"RDRM20060 - Domicile: Introduction and Background: Domicile and Law Territories,"* (GOV.UK, HMRC internal manual), accessed on July 5, 2019, https://www.gov.uk/hmrc-internal-manuals/residence-domicile-and-remittance-basis/rdrm20060

[33] *"Moving or returning to Ireland,"* (Revenue, Irish Tax and Customs), accessed on 5 July 2019, https://www.revenue.ie/en/life-events-and-personal-circumstances/moving-to-or-from-ireland/moving-or-returning-to-ireland/domicile-levy.aspx

[34] *"Taxation Ruling IT 2650, Income tax: residency - permanent place of abode outside Australia,"* NO 85/4612-6, (Australian Tax Office), https://www.ato.gov.au/law/view/document?Docid=ITR/IT2650/NAT/ATO/00 001:

"The terms "resident" and "resident of Australia" are defined in subsection 6(1) of the Income Tax Assessment Act 1936. So far as an individual is concerned, these terms are defined to mean:

(a) a person, other than a company, who resides in Australia and includes a person-

> *i. whose domicile is in Australia, unless the Commissioner is satisfied that his permanent place of abode is outside Australia;*
> *ii. who has actually been in Australia, continuously or intermittently, during more than one-half of the year of income, unless the Commissioner is satisfied that his usual place of abode is outside Australia and that he does not intend to take up residence in Australia; or*

iii. who is an eligible employee for the purposes of the Superannuation Act 1976 or is the spouse or a child under 16 years of age of such a person;"

[35] EY, *"Worldwide Personal Tax and Immigration Guide 2018-2019,"* (EY, 2018), https://webforms.ey.com/GL/en/Services/Tax/Global-tax-guide-archive.: *"Individuals are considered resident for tax purposes if they are present in Indonesia for more than 183 days within a 12-month period or if, within the calendar tax year, they reside in Indonesia with the intent to stay."*

[36] EY (2018), page 657: In Sri Lanka, the 183 day rule is the only consideration. Page 324 States: *"individuals are considered resident for tax purposes if they are present in Sri Lanka for more than 183 days in a tax year. A resident guest and a dual citizen are subject to tax only on income derived in Sri Lanka."*

[37] EY (2018), page 569: *"Individuals earning income that arises in or is derived from a Hong Kong office or Hong Kong employment, or from services rendered in Hong Kong during visits of more than 60 days in any tax year, are subject to salaries tax."*

[38] EY (2018), page 432: *"Persons of French or foreign nationality are considered residents for tax purposes if their home, principal place of abode, professional activity or center of economic interest is located in France."*

[39] *"Algemene wet inzake rijksbelastingen,"* Artikel 4, lid 1, available at: https://maxius.nl/algemene-wet-inzake-rijksbelastingen/artikel4: *"Waar iemand woont en waar een lichaam gevestigd is, wordt naar de omstandigheden beoordeeld."*

[40] *"Overige bezittingen,"* (Belasting Dienst), accessed on August 23, 2020, https://www.belastingdienst.nl/wps/wcm/connect/bldcontentnl/belastingdienst/prive/vermogen_en_aanmerkelijk_belang/vermogen/wat_zijn_uw_bezittingen_en_schulden/uw_bezittingen/overige_bezittingen/, [Author translation] *"Other assets include: cryptocurrency, such as bitcoins and other virtual payment methods."*

[41] Rothbard, Murray N. *"Jean-Baptiste Colbert and Louis XIV,"* (Mises.org, November 2, 2017), accessed on July 27, 2019, https://mises.org/library/jean-baptiste-colbert-and-louis-xiv

[42] *"Tax Withholding,"* (Amazon, Kindle Direct Publishing), accessed on July 5, 2019, https://kdp.amazon.com/en_US/help/topic/G201274690: *"Royalty payments for sales on the U.S. store are subject to 30% U.S. tax withholding, including payments from the KDP Select Global Fund. Publishers may be eligible for a reduced rate of U.S. tax withholding if their country of permanent residence has an income tax treaty with the United States. See the IRS website for a list of countries the U.S. has tax treaties with and for a table of tax treaty rates."*

[43] *"VAT rules for supplies of digital services to consumers in the EU,"* (GOV.UK, Guidance), accessed on July 2015, https://www.gov.uk/guidance/the-vat-rules-if-you-supply-digital-services-to-private-consumers#businesses-established-outside-the-eu: *"If you are based outside the EU and supply digital services to consumers in the EU, the place of supply will be where the consumer is located.*

You'll either have to:
* register for the VAT Mini One Stop Shop (VAT MOSS) in an EU member State
* register in each EU member State where your consumers are located"

[44] OECD, *"Model Tax Convention on Income and on Capital 2017 (Full Version),"* (OECD Publishing, Paris), https://read.oecd-ilibrary.org/taxation/model-tax-convention-on-income-and-on-capital-2017-full-version_g2g972ee-en#page49, page 49

[45] OECD, *"Interpretation And Application Of Article 5 (Permanent Establishment) Of The OECD Model Tax Convention,"* (OECD, Centre For Tax Policy And Administration, Paris, 12 October 2011 to 10 February 2012), http://www.oecd.org/tax/treaties/48836726.pdf, page 15:
"Whilst the practices followed by Member countries have not been consistent in so far as time requirements are concerned, experience has shown that permanent establishments normally have not been considered to exist in situations where a business had been carried on in a country through a place of business that was maintained for less than six months."

[46] Finnerty C.J., Merks P., et al, (2007), page 212

[47] Finnerty C.J., Merks P., et al, (2007), page 207

[48] *"Bank recovery and resolution,"* (European Commission, Policies, information and services), accessed on July 6, 2019, https://ec.europa.eu/info/business-economy-euro/banking-and-finance/financial-supervision-and-risk-management/managing-risks-banks-and-financial-institutions/bank-recovery-and-resolution_en

[49] Hill, Dr. W.G., *"PT: A Coherent for a Stress-free, Healthy and Properous Life Without Government Interference, Taxes or Coercion,"* (Expatworld, 1998), page 9:
"'About 20 years ago, I put the concept of PT into a mini-book I called How to Keep Your Money and Your Freedom. 'Three Flags' was the way I described the need to have a second passport, a safe haven for your assets outside your own country and a legal address in a tax haven. Over the following years, I wrote many newsletter segments about what I eventually came to call PT. It was also at about this time that I first met Bill Hill and with him expanded the three flags to five. We included a place of business and playgrounds. A consistent purpose in life is also one of the goals of the true PT. With the help of Bill Hill and others, I think I've discovered one answer to the question of how to live life to the fullest. Best wishes.'Harry D (for Dynamic) Schultz"

[50] Kalogerou D., *"Common and recurring weaknesses and/or deficiencies and best practice standards identified during the onsite inspections performed in relation to the prevention of money laundering and terrorist financing,"* Circular No C260, (Cyprus Securities and Exchange Commission, January 23, 2018), https://www.cysec.gov.cy/CMSPages/GetFile.aspx?guid=67566197-8896-4544-b0fd-69c772c5e873.
[Author note] With the bail-out of Cyprus the EU attached a requirement of stricter regulation of the financial services industry in Cyprus. I found this guidance illustrative because it spells out what "regulated entities" are required to do to monitor "suspicious" behavior (aka police their customers). Similar legislation is enforced all around the Western world.

[51] *"International Taxation,"* (Wikipedia), accessed on July 27, 2019, https://en.wikipedia.org/wiki/International_taxation#Individuals

[52] Finnerty C.J., Merks P., et al, (2007), page 6

[53] Idib., page 6

[54] EY (2018), page 1452:
"All resident and nonresident individuals earning income from sources in Thailand are subject to personal income tax (PIT). A Thai resident is also subject to PIT on self-employment and business income from sources overseas if the income is remitted to Thailand."

[55] *"Deemed Domicile rules,"* (GOV.UK, January 31, 2018),accessed on August 12, 2019, https://www.gov.uk/guidance/deemed-domicile-rules:
"If you aren't domiciled in the UK under English common law you're treated as domiciled in the UK for all tax purposes if either Condition A or Condition B is met."
"Condition B is met when you've been UK resident for at least 15 of the 20 tax years immediately before the relevant tax year."

[56] *"Swiss review tax breaks for rich foreigners,"* (IFC Review, April 7, 2011), accessed on July 7, 2019, http://www.ifcreview.com/viewarticle.aspx?articleId=3159&areaId=38.

[57] PWC, *"Europe's best kept secret - Individual Taxation,"* (Pricewaterhouse Coopers & Associados, 2014), https://www.pwc.pt/pt/fiscalidade/imagens/pwc_europe_best_kept_secret.pdf.

[58] *"Autoridade Tributária e Aduaneira, Tributação das cripto-moedas ou moedas virtuais,"* (Portal das Finanças, 27-12-2016), https://info.portaldasfinancas.gov.pt/pt/informacao_fiscal/informacoes_vinculativas/rendimento/cirs/Documents/PIV_09541.pdf.
[Author note]: This document lists three types of taxes: category G (capital gains), category E (capital income), and category B (business or professional income). It then explains how the sale of crypto-currencies doesn't fall in any of those categories, *"unless by its habituality it constitutes a professional or business activity of the taxpayer, in which case it will be taxed in category B."* (Translation provided to me by a tax inspector working at the AT).

[59] EY (2018), page 616, Rates:
"The taxation of Hungarian residents and foreign individuals is described below:
A 15% flat personal income tax rate applies to both the consolidated tax base and investment income.
Nonresidents are subject to tax on income derived from Hungarian sources at the rates that apply to residents."

[60] *"The SRRVisa,"* (Philippine Retirement Authority), accessed on July 7, 2019, https://pra.gov.ph/srrv/.

[61] These are the requirements for Bulgaria (where I have helped people obtain residency), and the Netherlands. The current requirements should always be checked for your situation.

[62] EY (2018), page 499:
"Individuals are subject to tax on their worldwide income if they meet either of the following conditions:
* They have a domicile in Germany for their personal use.

* *They have a 'customary place of abode' in Germany and do not stay only temporarily at this place or in this area. This means that if they are present in Germany for an uninterrupted period of at least six months that may fall in two calendar years, a customary place of abode is given in any case."*

[63] RDR3: Statutory Residence Test, (GOV.UK, HM Revenue & Customs, June 30, 2014), https://assets.publishing.service.gov.uk/government/uploads/system/uploads/attachment_data/file/547118/160803_RDR3_August2016_v2_0final_078500.pdf, page 9.

[64] EY (2018), page 445.

[65] Ibid., page 1366.

[66] Ibid., page 720.

[67] OECD *"Model Tax Convention on Income and on Capital 2017 (Full Version),"* (2017), p 45, Article 4, 2a:
"he shall be deemed to be a resident only of the State in which he has a permanent home available to him; if he has a permanent home available to him in both States, he shall be deemed to be a resident only of the State with which his personal and economic relations are closer (centre of vital interests);"

[68] *"Dispositions of property,"* (Government of Canada), accessed on July 7, 2019, https://www.canada.ca/en/revenue-agency/services/tax/international-non-residents/individuals-leaving-entering-canada-non-residents/dispositions-property.html.

[69] *"Combatting tax crimes,"* (Government of Canada website), accessed on August 15, 2020, https://www.canada.ca/en/revenue-agency/programs/about-canada-revenue-agency-cra/compliance/combat-tax-crimes.html

[70] Djelic, Marie-Laure, *"When Limited Liability was (Still) an Issue: Mobilization and Politics of Signification in 19th-Century England,"* (Sage Journals, Vol 34, Issue 5-6, 2013), http://journals.sagepub.com/doi/abs/10.1177/0170840613479223?journalCode=ossa, page 2.

[71] *"Parent companies and their subsidiaries in the European Union,"* (European Commission, Policies, information and services), accessed on July 7, 2019, https://ec.europa.eu/taxation_customs/business/company-tax/parent-companies-their-subsidiaries-eu-union_en:
"The 1990 Directive was designed to eliminate tax obstacles in the area of profit distributions between groups of companies in the EU by:
* abolishing withholding taxes on payments of dividends between associated companies of different Member States and
* preventing double taxation of parent companies on the profits of their subsidiaries."

[72] *"Automatic Exchange Portal, Online support for the implementation of automatic exchange of information in tax matters,"* (OECD), accessed on July 27, 2019, https://www.oecd.org/tax/automatic-exchange/common-reporting-standard/:
"The Common Reporting Standard (CRS), developed in response to the G20 request and approved by the OECD Council on 15 July 2014, calls on jurisdictions to obtain information from their

financial institutions and automatically exchange that information with other jurisdictions on an annual basis."

[73] Nestmann, M., *"The Lifeboat Strategy, 4th Edition (2011-2012),"* (API, Ltd. dba The Nestmann Group, Ltd., February 26, 2009), page 106.

[74] *"Types of Suspicious Activities or Transactions,"* (FIU FRAUD ALERT), accessed on August 23, 2020, http://fiubelize.org/types-of-suspicious-activities-or-transactions/. [Author Note]: think for example about how common the following is for a CI:
* *"Reluctance to provide normal information when opening an account, providing minimal or fictitious information or, when applying to open an account, providing information that is difficult or expensive for the institution to verify;"*
* *"Clients with distant addresses who could find the same services nearer their home base."*
* *"Building up of large balances, not consistent with the known turnover of the customer's business, and subsequent transfer to account(s) held overseas;"*
* *"Insufficient use of normal banking facilities."*
* *"Any transaction in which the counterparty to the transaction is unknown." [to the institution]*
* *"Any transaction in which the nature, size or frequency appears unusual."*
* *"Unwillingness to disclose the source of funds."*

[75] Huillet, M., *"Silk Road Prosecutor: 99.9% of Fiat Money Laundering Goes Unprosecuted,"* (Cointelegraph, Oct 22, 2019), accessed on August 23, 2020, https://cointelegraph.com/news/silk-road-prosecutor-999-of-fiat-money-laundering-goes-unprosecuted.

[76] [Author Note] During my studies we had a lecture from a surprisingly honest banker of ING, who told us they provided extremely risky loans for real estate deals because they knew the government/tax payers would bail them out. "Now it's your problem" he said. As an example of a risky loan he told how a notary refused a transaction of a property in Germany, because both the bank and the buyer had never seen it. It turned out to be a complete dump. But yeah, I am a "high risk" to ING because I live in Asia.

[77] [Author note] A fiscally transparent entity is disregarded for tax purposes in the country of registration (subject to limitations, such as no local sourced income). The income generated in such entities is taxed at the level of the shareholder. If you live in the West, such income is taxed at the highest brackets. If you pay no or little income tax, this is a way to use business registrations in Western countries to enjoy the benefits of access to the financial system while staying tax efficient.

[78] *"List of Third Parties (other than PayPal Customers) with Whom Personal Information May be Shared,"* (Paypal, July 1, 2019), accessed on July 7, 2019, https://www.paypal.com/uk/webapps/mpp/ua/third-parties-list

[79] You can setup a self-hosted payment server by using open source software to start accepting Bitcoin payments. It can integrated with a number of payment processors. It's secure, private, censorship-resistant and free. More info here: https://btcpayserver.org/.

[80] *"History of the Internet,"* (Wikipedia), accessed Aug 18, 2018, https://en.wikipedia.org/wiki/History_of_the_Internet

[81] *"What Is the Lightning Network?"* (Bitcoin Magazine), accessed on August 21, 2020, https://bitcoinmagazine.com/what-is-bitcoin/what-is-the-lightning-network:
"The Lightning Network is a "layer two" protocol for Bitcoin, specifically designed for cheap, fast and private payments. As an overlay network consisting of payment channels, Lightning payments are not recorded on Bitcoin's blockchain — only channel-funding transactions and channel-closing transactions are. This effectively means that many Lightning transactions can be settled with much fewer on-chain Bitcoin transactions."

[82] Vanham, P., *"Global Pension Timebomb: Funding Gap Set to Dwarf World GDP,"* (World Economic Forum, May 26, 2017), accessed on July 28, 2019, https://www.weforum.org/press/2017/05/global-pension-timebomb-funding-gap-set-to-dwarf-world-gdp:
"The world's six largest pension saving systems—the US, UK, Japan, Netherlands, Canada and Australia—are expected to reach a $224 trillion gap by 2050, a new study by the World Economic Forum shows."
[Author note: don't worry, YOUR pension will be fine...]

[83] *"clogs to clogs in three generations,"* (Wikipedia), accessed on July 7, 2019, https://en.wiktionary.org/wiki/clogs_to_clogs_in_three_generations

[84] *"Convention on the Recognition and Enforcement of Foreign Arbitral Awards,"* (United Nations, New York, 1958), accessed April 6, 2018, https://treaties.un.org/doc/Treaties/1959/06/19590607%2009-35%20PM/Ch_XXII_01p.pdf.

[85] Darwin C., *"On the Origin of Species: By Means of Natural Selection or the Preservation of Favoured Races in the Struggle for Life,"* (1859), http://www.vliz.be/docs/Zeecijfers/Origin_of_Species.pdf, page 43:
"When we see leaf-eating insects green, and bark-feeders mottled-grey; the alpine ptarmigan white in winter, the red-grouse the colour of heather, and the black-grouse that of peaty earth, we must believe that these tints are of service to these birds and insects in preserving them from danger. Grouse, if not destroyed at some period of their lives, would increase in countless numbers; they are known to suffer largely from birds of prey; and hawks are guided by eyesight to their prey,--so much so, that on parts of the Continent persons are warned not to keep white pigeons, as being the most liable to destruction. Hence I can see no reason to doubt that natural selection might be most effective in giving the proper colour to each kind of grouse, and in keeping that colour, when once acquired, true and constant."

[86] *"Madoff investment scandal,"* (Wikipedia), accessed on July 7, 2019, https://en.wikipedia.org/wiki/Madoff_investment_scandal:
"Rather than offer high returns to all comers, Madoff offered modest but steady returns to an exclusive clientele. The investment method was marketed as 'too complicated for outsiders to understand'. He was secretive about the firm's business, and kept his financial Statements closely guarded.[43] The New York Post reported that Madoff 'worked the so-called Jewish circuit of well-heeled Jews he met at country clubs on Long Island and in Palm Beach'."

[87] [Author note] One of the more successful pyramid scams has been Onecoin, promoted by a Bulgarian woman named Ruja Ignatova. She is now (April, 2020) on the run for law enforcement, her brother and others participants have been convicted for their role in this cryptocurrency pyramid scam.

Read more here: https://www.bbc.com/news/technology-50417908

[88] *"Sri Lanka: Muslims Face Threats, Attacks"* (Human Rights Watch, July 3, 2019), accessed on July 2019, https://www.hrw.org/news/2019/07/04/sri-lanka-muslims-face-threats-attacks.

[89] Yan, A., *"Pollution claims 1.8 million lives in China, latest research says,"* (South China Morning Post, October 20, 2017), accessed on July 27, 2019, https://www.scmp.com/news/china/society/article/2116342/pollution-claims-18-million-lives-china-latest-research-says.

[90] *"Citizenship,"* (Encyclopedia Britannica), access on July 9, 2019, https://www.britannica.com/topic/citizenship

[91] League of Nations, *"Convention on Certain Questions Relating to the Conflict of Nationality Laws,"* (The League of Nations Codification Conference, The Hague, 1930), http://eudo-citizenship.eu/InternationalDB/docs/Convention%20on%20certain%20questions%20relating%20to%20the%20conflict%20of%20nationality%20laws%20FULL%20TEXT.pdf.

[92] OECD, *"Naturalisation: A Passport for the Better Integration of Immigrants?,"* (OECD, Paris, 2011), https://read.oecd-ilibrary.org/social-issues-migration-health/naturalisation-a-passport-for-the-better-integration-of-immigrants_9789264099104-en#page70, page 70.

[93] Jorden M., *"3 Arrested in Crackdown on Multimillion-Dollar 'Birth Tourism' Businesses"* (The New York Times, Jan 31, 2019), accessed on July 7, 2019, https://www.nytimes.com/2019/01/31/us/anchor-baby-birth-tourism.html.

[94] OECD (2011), *"Naturalisation: A Passport for the Better Integration of Immigrants?,"* page 71-74.

[95] Chu, B., *"What are 'golden passport' schemes and how do they enable tax dodging?"* (Independent), accessed on July 28, 2019, https://www.independent.co.uk/news/business/analysis-and-features/golden-passports-explained-visas-oecd-tax-dodging-investors-a8587051.html

[96] Evans, Malcolm D. *"International Law, 3rd Edition"* (Oxford University Press, 2010), page 7:
"Much of State practice in the Middle Ages consisted of traditional ways inherited from ancient times. The area of diplomatic relations is an example, with diplomats increasing being accorded a broad (but not absolute) degree of immunity from judicial process in host States."

[97] Evans, *"International Law, 3rd Edition"* (Oxford University Press, 2010), page 382:
"The first is immunity {ratione personae}, ie immunities enjoyed by certain categories of State officials by virtue of their office. These immunities are often wide enough to cover both the official and the private acts of such office-holders, since interference with the performance of the official functions of such a person can result from the subjection of either type of act to the jurisdiction of the receiving State."
page 383: *"The second type of immunity {ratione materiae} - these immunities attach to the official*

acts of State officials. They are determined by reference to the nature of the acts in question, rather than by reference to the particular office of the official who performed them."

[98] UN, *"Vienna Convention on Diplomatic Relations,"* (United Nations,Vienna, 1961), http://legal.un.org/ilc/texts/instruments/english/conventions/9_1_1961.pdf:
* Article 27: a diplomatic bag must never be opened.
* Article 33: exemption from social security.
* Article 34: exemption from taxes.
* Article 36: exemption from customs duties.

[99] FATF, *"Politically Exposed Persons (recommendations 12 and 22),"* (Financial Action Task Force, Paris, 2013), http://www.fatf-gafi.org/media/fatf/documents/recommendations/Guidance-PEP-Rec12-22.pdf, Page 6: **Foreign PEPs**: *"individuals who are or have been entrusted with prominent public functions by a foreign country, for example Heads of State or of government, senior politicians, senior government, judicial or military officials, senior executives of State owned corporations, important political party officials."*
Page 7: *"Foreign PEPs are always considered high risk and require the application of enhanced due diligence measures."*
page 12: *"Recommendation 12 applies also to family members and close associates of the PEP."*

[100] *"United Nations laissez-passer,"* (Wikipedia), accessed on July 9, 2019, https://en.wikipedia.org/wiki/United_Nations_laissez-passer.

[101] *"Supplementary Protocol No. 1 to the Convention for European Economic Co-operation on the Legal Capacity, Privileges and Immunities of the Organisation,"* (Convention for European Economic Cooperation, Paris, April 16, 1948), accessed on July 9, 2019, http://www.oecd.org/general/supplementaryprotocolno1totheconventionforeuropeaneconomicco-operationonthelegalcapacityprivilegesandimmunitiesoftheorganisation.htm:
*"Article 6 - The Organisation, its assets, income and other property shall be:
(a) exempt from all direct taxes; it is understood, however, that the Organisation will not claim exemption from rates and taxes which are in fact no more than charges for public utility services;
(b) exempt from customs duties and prohibitions and restrictions on imports and exports in respect of articles imported or exported by the Organisation for its official use. It is understood however that articles imported under such exemption will not be sold in the country into which they were imported except under conditions agreed with the Government of that country;
(c) exempt from customs duties and prohibitions and restrictions on imports and exports in respect of its publications."*

[102] Chapelle, B. de la, Fehlinger, P., *"Jurisdiction On The Internet: From Legal Arms Race To Transnational Cooperation,"* (Internet & Jurisdiction, April 2016), accessed on July 9, 2019, https://www.internetjurisdiction.net/uploads/pdfs/Papers/IJ-Paper-Jurisdiction-on-the-Internet-PDF.pdf

[103] Rosenberg, P., *"The Insider's Guide to Online Privacy - A Freeman's Perspective Special Report,"* (Cryptohippie USA).

[104] Jokinen K., Nilsson L., *"Server holdings may entail a permanent establishment,"* (PWC, Tax matters - Sweden's tax blog), accessed July 9, 2019,

https://blogg.pwc.se/taxmatters-en/server-holdings-may-entail-a-permanent-establishment

[105] [Author note: The UK has a straightforward system determining when you don't have to pay taxes, mostly determined by the amount of days you spend in the country. The HMRS confirmed this by phone to two clients of mine.

[106] IRS, *"Publication 54 - Tax Guide for U.S. Citizens and Resident Aliens Abroad - Fur use in preparing 2018 Returns,"* (Department of the Treasury, Internal Revenue Service, 2018), https://www.irs.gov/pub/irs-pdf/p54.pdf

[107] IRS, *"Form 1040 and 1040-SR Instructions,"* (Department of the Treasury, Internal Revenue Service, 2019), https://www.irs.gov/pub/irs-pdf/i1040gi.pdf, page 6.

[108] IRS, *"Schedule 1, Additional Income and Adjustments to Income,"* (Department of the Treasury, Internal Revenue Service, 2019), https://www.irs.gov/pub/irs-pdf/f1040s1.pdf.
[Author note: I saw a video of someone claiming that from 2020 onwards this checkbox is found on the main form, emphasizing how seriousness the IRS take crypto-currencies].

[109] IRS, *"Notice 2014-21,"* (Department of the Treasury, Internal Revenue Service, 2014), https://www.irs.gov/pub/irs-drop/n-14-21.pdf, page 2, Section 4, Frequently Asked Questions.

[110] Ibid., page 1, Section 3, Scope.

[111] Ibid., page 1, Section 2, Background.

[112] IRS, *"Form 8949, Sales and Other Dispositions of Capital Assets,"* (Department of the Treasury, Internal Revenue Service, 2019), https://www.irs.gov/pub/irs-pdf/f8949.pdf.

[113] IRS, *"SCHEDULE D, Capital Gains and Losses,"* (Department of the Treasury, Internal Revenue Service, 2019), https://www.irs.gov/pub/irs-pdf/f1040sd.pdf.

[114] IRS, *"Report of Foreign Bank and Financial Accounts (FBAR),"* (IRS), accessed on July 10, 2019, https://www.irs.gov/businesses/small-businesses-self-employed/report-of-foreign-bank-and-financial-accounts-fbar.

[115] *"Do I need to file Form 8938, 'Statement of Specified Foreign Financial Assets?'"* (IRS), accessed on July 10, 2019, https://www.irs.gov/businesses/corporations/do-i-need-to-file-form-8938-Statement-of-specified-foreign-financial-assets:
"A specified individual is:
* A U.S. citizen.
* A resident alien of the United States for any part of the tax year (see Publication 519 for more information).
* A nonresident alien who makes an election to be treated as resident alien for purposes of filing a joint income tax return.
* A nonresident alien who is a bona fide resident of American Samoa or Puerto Rico (See Publication 570 for definition of a bona fide resident)."

116 *"Summary of FATCA Reporting for U.S. Taxpayers,"* (IRS), accessed on August 23, 2020, https://www.irs.gov/businesses/corporations/summary-of-fatca-reporting-for-us-taxpayers:
"Taxpayers living abroad. You must file a Form 8938 if you must file an income tax return and:
* You are not a married person filing a joint income tax return and the total value of your specified foreign financial assets is more than $200,000 on the last day of the tax year or more than $300,000 at any time during the year."

117 *"Summary of FATCA Reporting for U.S. Taxpayers,"* (IRS):
"If you must file Form 8938 and do not do so, you may be subject to penalties: a $10,000 failure to file penalty, an additional penalty of up to $50,000 for continued failure to file after IRS notification, and a 40 percent penalty on an underStatement of tax attributable to non-disclosed assets."

118 [Author note] For now *not* reportable!

119 IRS, *"Publication 54,"* (2018), page 12

120 Ibid., page 12

121 Ibid., page 16

122 Ibid., page 16

123 Ibid., page 16

124 Ibid., page 21

125 *"Topic Number 856 - Foreign Tax Credit,"* (IRS), accessed on July 11, 2019, https://www.irs.gov/taxtopics/tc856.

126 World Health Organization, *"International health regulations (2005) -- 2 nd ed.,"* (WHO, 2008), https://www.who.int/ihr/9789241596664/en/:
[Author note] this document, signed by 196 States, clearly spells out that the WHO can declare an emergency (Article 12 & 49), after witch it can make temporary (Article 15) and standing (Article 16) "recommendations" regarding "persons" amongst others: isolate, quarantine, refuse to travel (entry/exit), contact tracing, and obligatory vaccination.

Made in the USA
Coppell, TX
19 August 2021